COLLECTIONS

Practice Book
Grade 1

Welcome Home

Set Sail

Harcourt

Orlando   Boston   Dallas   Chicago   San Diego

Visit *The Learning Site!*

www.harcourtschool.com

Contents

Contents

SET SAIL

Contents

Welcome
Home

Name _____

▶ **Look at each picture. Write the word in the box that completes the sentence.**

| green | bee | eat | seat | me | feet |

1. The cat is on the _____.

2. She sees the _____.

3. She lands on her _____.

4. She wants to _____.

5. Her rug is _____.

She comes to _____.

6.

SCHOOL-HOME CONNECTION Write the words. Ask your child to circle the words with *ee* and to draw a line under the words with *ea*. Then let him or her read the words.

Name _____

► **Write the name of the holiday that matches each clue. Begin each holiday name with a capital letter.**

valentine's day

new year's day

thanksgiving day

I. We make cards for friends. We use red.

_____

- -

_____

2. This is the first day of the year!

_____

- -

_____

3. We give thanks this day.

_____

- -

_____

TRY THIS Write about your favorite holiday. Draw a picture to go with your story.

SCHOOL-HOME CONNECTION Look at a calendar with your child. Review the holidays and special days for each month.

Welcome Home
Lesson 1

9

Harcourt

▶ **Write the word that best completes each sentence.**

full	should	room	Try	moved

_____

Cat came into the _____. I

_____

_____ her bowl down. Her dish

_____

was _____. "You

_____

_____ eat," I said.

"It's good.

_____

_____ some."

▶ **Write the word that best completes
each sentence.**

hear	only	Please	write	full

_____

Now my cat is _____ .

_____

I _____ her. She is happy.

_____

She likes it. I _____ "yes."

_____

" _____ get more for my cat."

_____

If _____ she liked all

her food.

TRY THIS Use some of the words from the box to write a note
to a friend. Then circle the words you picked.

SCHOOL-HOME CONNECTION Ask your child to read each
sentence of the story.

Welcome Home
Lesson 2

11

Harcourt

Name _____

▶ **Do what each sentence tells you. Then circle the words that contain vowel ē.**

1. A cat eats a sweet treat. Color the ice cream.

2. One cat feels the heat. Color this cat pink.

3. A teeny cat sees the fish. Color this cat green.

4. The cat cleans its feet. Color this cat yellow.

5. Three cats seem tired. They want to sleep.
   Color them red.

6. A cat reads to me. Color its feet.

SCHOOL-HOME CONNECTION Write the long vowel *e* words in the sentences on small cards. Have your child read the words and catergorize them according to the spelling (*e, ee, ea*).

Harcourt

Name _____

▶ **Write the spelling word in the box that tells about the picture.**

we	see	eat	read	me

1.

_____

- - - - - - - - - - -

_____

2.

_____

- - - - - - - - - - -

_____

3.

_____

- - - - - - - - - - -

_____

4.

_____

- - - - - - - - - - -

_____

5.

_____

- - - - - - - - - - -

_____

Harcourt

SCHOOL-HOME CONNECTION Cut out 14 small squares. Write one letter on each square: 6 *e*'s, 2 *a*'s, 1 *w*, 1 *s*, 1 *t*, 1 *d*, 1 *m*, and 1 *r*. Then turn them over and take turns picking a letter until you can make a spelling word.

Name _____

▶ **Think about what happened in the story.
Then complete the flowchart.**

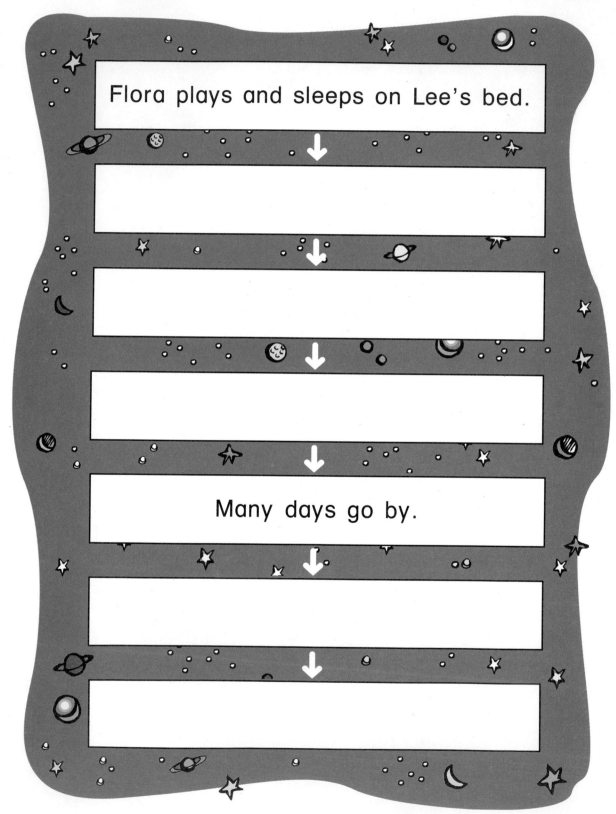

Flora plays and sleeps on Lee's bed.

⬇

⬇

⬇

Many days go by.

⬇

⬇

Welcome Home
Lesson 2

SCHOOL-HOME CONNECTION Have your child retell the
story, using the flowchart to tell the events in order.

Harcourt

▶ **Draw a picture to show what happens next.**

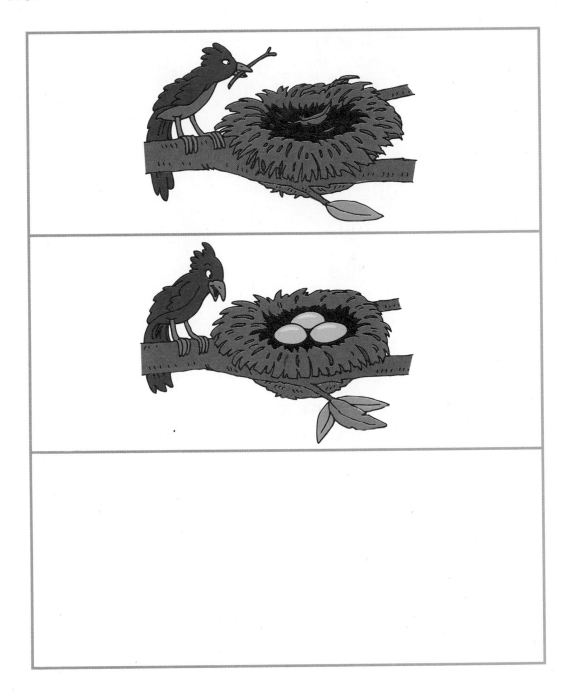

 TRY THIS Write sentences to go with your story.

SCHOOL-HOME CONNECTION Ask your child to tell you a story about the pictures.

Welcome Home
Lesson 3   15

Harcourt

Name _____

▶ **Look at the pictures. Then choose the best answer. Fill in the oval next to your answer.**

1. What will happen next?

⬭ Snow will fall.

⬭ The man will play.

⬭ The snow will melt.

⬭ The man will grow.

▶ **Choose the best answer. Fill in the circle next to your answer.**

2. What will happen next?

⬭ He will get a haircut.

⬭ He will eat lunch.

⬭ He will read a book.

⬭ He will brush his teeth.

Harcourt

Name _____

▶ **Write the word that best completes each sentence.**

flying   flies

_____

- - - - - - - - - - - - - - - -

1. She _____ away and comes back.

hunting   hunts

_____

- - - - - - - - - - - - - - - -

2. She _____ for soft

things to pad the nest.

carry   carries

_____

- - - - - - - - - - - - - - - -

3. She _____ them

back to the nest.

tried   trying

_____

- - - - - - - - - - - - - - - -

4. She _____ to make

a good nest.

SCHOOL-HOME CONNECTION Together, write a list of words that end in -s, -ed, and -es. Take turns making up a sentence with each word.

Harcourt

Name _____

▶ **Use the word from the box that best completes each sentence. Then read the story.**

| Take | cake | gave | Kate | game | ate |

The Surprise

_____   _____

_____ is my friend. She _____

_____

me a map. "_____ this map, and find the

surprise." I walked all around the house.

_____

The _____ was fun. The surprise

_____

was a birthday _____.

_____

We _____ it all!

Welcome Home
Lesson 6

SCHOOL-HOME CONNECTION Read the words in the box. Ask your child to write *gave*, *game*, and *ate*. Then write two rhyming words for each.

Harcourt

Name _____

▶ **Read the story and complete the**
sentences with the words I or me.

_____

_____ like to go to the park with Doug. We

_____ _____

swing. Doug pushes _____. Then _____ push

_____

him. We play ball. _____ kick the ball to Doug. He

_____ _____

kicks the ball to _____. We climb. _____ go up to

_____

the top. _____ like to play at the park.

SCHOOL-HOME CONNECTION Ask your child to draw a picture of himself
or herself playing with a friend. Have your child write a caption using *I*.
Then have your child write a second caption using *me*.

Harcourt

▶ **Choose the word from the box that best completes each sentence.**

world	place	country	Earth	town
special		United States of America		

_____

1. My room is a _____ place.

_____

2. The _____ spins around the sun.

_____

3. The flag of the _____

_____

_____ has stars and stripes.

_____

4. What _____ do you live in?

Harcourt

Name _____

▶ **Read each clue. Write the word that solves the riddle.**

5. It is shaped like a ball. People live here. It's also called Earth.

_____

_____

6. Some people call it U.S.A. for short.

_____

_____

_____

_____

7. It's not the biggest place to live. People live, work, and shop here. It sounds like <u>down</u>.

_____

_____

_____

8. I am somewhere. I sound like <u>space</u>.

_____

_____

| TRY **⟋** THIS | Write the vocabulary words on separate pieces of paper. Put the words in order, from shortest to longest. |

Harcourt

SCHOOL-HOME CONNECTION Talk to your child about the names of your street, town, state, and country. Ask your child to address an envelope to themselves. Write him or her a special note and mail it.

Name _____

▶ **Use the words in the box. Write the word that names the picture.**

| shade | skate | lake | wave | grapes |

1. _____

2. _____

3. _____

4. _____

5. _____

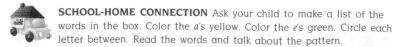

SCHOOL-HOME CONNECTION Ask your child to make a list of the words in the box. Color the *a*'s yellow. Color the *e*'s green. Circle each letter between. Read the words and talk about the pattern.

Harcourt

Name _____

▶ **Write the word that best completes each sentence.**

came	game	made	make	take

_____

– – – – – – – – – – – – – – –

1. Come play a _____ with us.

_____

– – – – – – – – – – – – – – –

2. We need to _____ a team.

_____

– – – – – – – – – – – – – – –

3. We _____ to give you a map.

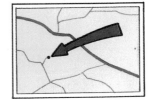

_____

– – – – – – – – – – – – – – –

4. We _____ it.

_____

– – – – – – – – – – – – – – –

5. It is faster if you _____ the bus.

Harcourt

TRY THIS Write a two-line poem about soccer. Use one or two spelling words.

SCHOOL-HOME CONNECTION Make pairs of words that sound the same. Add two more rhyming words to each pair.

Name _____

▶ **Think about the story. Think about the maps and the places on the maps. Write the places in order to complete the story chart.**

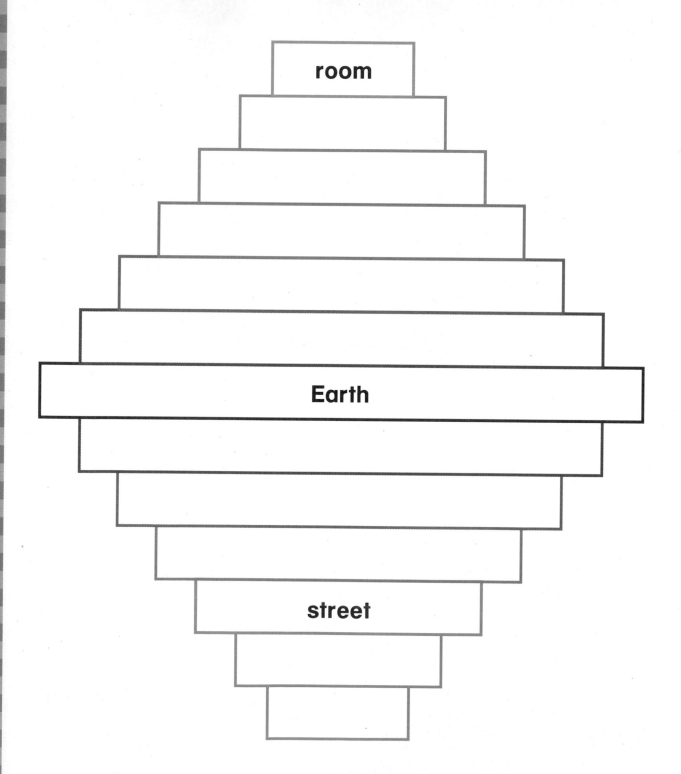

room

Earth

street

Welcome Home
Lesson 7

SCHOOL-HOME CONNECTION Help your child draw a map of his or her bedroom. Help your child label it and write his or her address on the other side.

Harcourt

Name _____

▶ **Look at Joey's picture and story. Write the word in the box that best completes each sentence.**

| sleeps | neat | clean | me | green | She |

_____

See _____ in my room? I can

_____   _____

_____ my room. I like it _____ .

_____

I have a _____ door. My dog

_____   _____

_____ in my room. _____

likes the soft rug.

SCHOOL-HOME CONNECTION Write the words as a list. Talk about the letters that stand for the long *e* sound. Let your child circle the *e*, *ee*, or *ea* in each word. Think of other long *e* words and write them.

Welcome Home
Lesson 8   25

Harcourt

Name _____

▶ **Read the story. Then answer the question.**

This is a map of the United States. It is a big country. It has many towns. There are 50 states. People live and work in every state. There is much to see in the United States.

What is this story about?

_____

- -

_____

_____

- -

_____

SCHOOL-HOME CONNECTION Tell your child a story about a move you made. Ask him or her to draw a picture of your story.

Harcourt

Name _____

▶ **Read each story. Then choose the best answer. Fill in the oval next to your answer.**

Owls are night birds. Some are big and some are small. They hunt at night. They catch mice and small animals. They sleep in the day.

1. What is this story about?
   - ○ It is about mice.
   - ○ It is about night.
   - ○ It is about owls.
   - ○ It is about sleep.

Many animals hatch from eggs. Birds and ducks hatch from eggs. Frogs and snakes hatch from eggs. Bugs hatch from eggs, too.

2. What is this story about?
   - ○ It is about bugs.
   - ○ It is about ducks.
   - ○ It is about animals that swim.
   - ○ It is about animals that hatch.

Harcourt

Name _____

▶ **Write the word that best completes each sentence.**

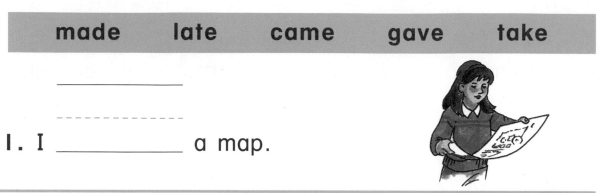

| made | late | came | gave | take |

_____

- - - - - - - - - - -

1. I _____ a map.

_____

- - - - - - - - - - -

2. I will _____ my map with me.

_____

- - - - - - - - - - -

3. Jenny _____ with me.

_____

- - - - - - - - - - -

4. We can't be _____!

_____

- - - - - - - - - - -

5. We _____ our maps to Mr. Smith.

 TRY THIS Make a list of words with the ending <u>-ake</u>. Compare your list with a partner.

🏠 **SCHOOL-HOME CONNECTION** Help your child write five new sentences using each word from the box above. Ask him or her to circle the vocabulary word in each sentence.

Harcourt

Name _____

▶ **Look at the picture. Follow the directions to finish the picture.**

1. Color the blocks green.

2. Make two more books on the shelf.

3. Put a boy on the horse.

4. Color the rug purple.

5. Color one ball red.

 TRY THIS Draw a picture for a friend. Write a sentence that tells your friend to do something to your picture. Watch your friend follow your directions.

 SCHOOL-HOME CONNECTION Give your child a blank sheet of paper and a crayon. Give one direction, like "draw a big circle" or "fold the paper in half." Then you take the paper, and let your child give you a direction.

Welcome Home
Lesson 9   29

Harcourt

Name _____

► **Read Ann's list. Circle the words that sound like <u>cake</u>.**

1. Cut apples to make a pie.

2. Bake the pie.

3. Go outside and shake the rug.

4. Take out the trash.

► **Draw a line under the words that sound like <u>late</u>.**

5. Open the gate.

6. Get a plate for each of us.

7. Call Kate to come.

8. Then eat the pie and go skate with Kate!

 TRY THIS Make a list of the words that end with <u>ake</u>. Then make a list of the words that end with <u>ate</u>.

SCHOOL-HOME CONNECTION Ask your child to pick two words that rhyme from this page. Together, write a two-line poem.

Harcourt

▶ **Read the story. Circle the words with y or ie.**

This tiny spot on the map is our town. We are having a town birthday. Today the town is 100 years old. We are busy. We play games and tell stories. We eat pie and cake. We read very old newspapers. Everybody is happy because our town is really special.

Harcourt

SCHOOL–HOME CONNECTION With your child, make a list of the circled words. Read each word and have your child circle the y's and the ie's.

Welcome Home
Lesson 11
31

Name _____

▶ **Use a word from the box to complete each sentence. Circle the noun that the new word tells about.**

They	he	She	it

1. Is Tom home?

_____

- - - - - - - - - -

Can _____ play with us?

2. Does Tom have a bat?

_____

- - - - - - - - - -

He can bring _____ to play ball.

3. Bill and Pam are coming, too.

_____

- - - - - - - - - -

_____ will meet us at the park.

4. Mother will bring us home.

_____

- - - - - - - - - -

_____ can bring Tom home, too.

SCHOOL-HOME CONNECTION Write a sentence for your child. Read it aloud. Ask your child to change the noun to *he, she, it,* or *they*, and say the sentence again. Repeat to use each of the pronouns.

Harcourt

Name _____

▶ **Read the words in the box. Match each word to a clue. Write the word.**

| before | thought | nice | laugh | most | carry |

It's more than some.

_____

_ _ _ _ _ _ _ _ _ _

_____

I did think about it.

_____

_ _ _ _ _ _ _ _ _ _

Take it with you.

_____

_ _ _ _ _ _ _ _ _ _

You do this for fun.

_____

_ _ _ _ _ _ _ _ _ _

I am not mean.

_____

_ _ _ _ _ _ _ _ _ _

Not today, but yesterday.

_____

_ _ _ _ _ _ _ _ _ _

 TRY THIS Use words in the box to write three sentences. Then draw pictures to match your sentences.

Name _____

▶ **Read the words in the box. Write the word that completes the sentence.**

thought	nice	laugh	most	carry

_____

1. I _____ a new book

to my brother.

_____

2. He is very _____.

_____

3. We play _____ of the time.

_____

4. We _____ at the story.

_____

5. We _____ the book

was very good.

TRY THIS Write the word <u>nice</u>. Write a sentence with this word. Then draw a picture to go with your sentence.

SCHOOL-HOME CONNECTION Let your child pick out a favorite story book. Read it together.

Harcourt

Name _____

► **Read the paragraph. Find the words that have the long vowel e sound spelled y or ie. Circle them. Then write the words below.**

Most of the time my baby sister Katie is happy. I showed her how to sort blocks. She does it quickly now. When she's really hungry, she cries. That's what babies do best!

SCHOOL-HOME CONNECTION With your child, review the list. Have your child draw a line around the letters that stand for the long e sound

Welcome Home
Lesson 12

35

Harcourt

▶ **Write the word in the box that best completes the sentence.**

any	Katie	many	very	funny

_____

- - - - - - - - - - - - - - - -

1. I have _____ books to read.

_____

- - - - - - - - - - - - - - - -

2. Some books are _____ big.

_____

- - - - - - - - - - - - - - - -

3. I read to _____ .

_____

- - - - - - - - - - - - - - - -

4. Some stories are really _____ .

_____

- - - - - - - - - - - - - - - -

5. I do not have _____ books left.

SCHOOL-HOME CONNECTION Read picture books together, and try to find these spelling words on the pages.

Harcourt

Name _____

▶ **Think about Lilly's feelings during the story. Then complete the flowchart.**

1. Lilly is happy to see Katie.

2.

3.

4.

5.

6.

7.

8.

TRY THIS Add a new part to the story. Write about a few more ups and downs in Lilly's day.

SCHOOL-HOME CONNECTION Help your child write or draw a story sequence about an imaginary day when he or she has ups and downs.

Harcourt

Name _____

▶ **Use the words in the box. Write the word that best completes each sentence.**

garden	park	cart	car	yarn

_____

1. I go with Mom and Dad in the _____.

_____

2. We _____ the car.

_____

3. We get a _____.

_____

4. Mom gets red _____.

_____

5. Here is a plant for the _____.

TRY THIS Make a list of words that contain <u>ar</u>. Are the letters at the beginning, the end, or in the middle of the words?

SCHOOL-HOME CONNECTION Ask your child to read the words in the box. Have him or her circle the two letters that are the same in every word and then read the words again.

▶ **Read the story. Then answer the questions.**

Jack and his mother go to the beach. They walk on the hot sand. They get wet. They find small shells. They write in the sand. The beach is a nice place to play.

Main Idea
What is the story about?

↓

Details
What did you find out?

 TRY THIS Draw a picture of yourself at the beach or at a pool. Label five details in your picture.

 **SCHOOL-HOME CONNECTION** Talk about a recent trip you took with your child. Recall some of the details.

Name _____

▶ **Read each story. Then choose the best answer. Fill in the oval next to your answer.**

Lilly saw a kangaroo. The kangaroo had a baby with her. The baby kangaroo was brown and had a long tail. It could jump fast and far.

1. What did you learn about the kangaroo?
   - ⬭ It is small.
   - ⬭ It can jump far.
   - ⬭ It has long arms.
   - ⬭ It has a short tail.

Apples grow on trees. Apples can be green, red, or yellow. Some are sweet. Some are tart. Some are good to bake with. Others are better for eating fresh. Apples are ready to pick in the fall.

2. What did you learn about apples?
   - ⬭ Apples are always red.
   - ⬭ Apples are good in soup.
   - ⬭ Apple seeds are good to eat.
   - ⬭ You can bake some apples.

Harcourt

Name _____

▶ **Write the words in ABC order. One has been done for you in each set.**

laugh   yell   pick   duck

_____

1. _____   2. _____

3. _____   4. ___ *yell*

baby   happy   "outside   walk

_____

1. _____   2. *happy*

3. _____   4. _____

Harcourt

SCHOOL-HOME CONNECTION Write each of these words on a small card. Let your child pick three and put them in ABC order. Mix them and play again.

Name _____

▶ **Read each sentence. Combine the two words to form a contraction. Write the contraction to complete the sentence.**

She is

_____

1. _____ getting lots of nuts.

He is

_____

2. _____ busy, too.

do not

_____

3. They _____ eat them all now.

They will

_____

4. _____ put the nuts away.

SCHOOL-HOME CONNECTION Make a list of these contractions with your child. Next to each contraction, ask your child to write the two words that make up the contraction.

Harcourt

▶ **Write the word in the box that best completes each sentence in the story.**

feet	sweet	meet	feed

_____

I _____ Mitch

every Monday. We like to get our

_____

_____ wet in the pond. We like to

_____

_____ the ducks. On the way home

_____

we get a _____ treat.

Name _____

▶ **Solve each riddle. Write the words in the puzzle.**

five	bike	smile	white	slide	time

2. ↓

1. →

3. ↓

4. ↓

5. →

6. →

1.	the color of snow
2.	use a clock to tell _ _ _ _
3.	two-wheeler
4.	seen on a happy face
5.	ride down the _ _ _ _ _
6.	5

SCHOOL-HOME CONNECTION Have your child
write a rhyming word for each word in the puzzle.

Harcourt

Name _____

▶ **Look at the pictures and write a word that describes the feeling.**

| happy | hungry | sad | surprised | tired |

1. _____   2. _____

3. _____

4. _____   5. _____

SCHOOL-HOME CONNECTION With your child, think of other words that describe feelings. Have your child draw a picture of one new word.

Welcome Home
Lesson 16   **45**

Harcourt

Name _____

▶ **Write the word that completes each sentence. Read the story when you are finished.**

My Fishing Story

<u>gone   together</u>

- - - - - - - - - - - - - - - - - -

1. Dad and I fish _____ .

<u>once   sound</u>

- - - - - - - - - - - - - - - - - -

2. We like the _____ of the water.

<u>sound   while</u>

- - - - - - - - - - - - - - - - - -

3. I whistle _____ I fish.

<u>Once   While</u>

- - - - - - - - - - - - - - - - - -

4. _____ I saw lots of fish.

<u>gone   bears</u>

- - - - - - - - - - - - - - - - - -

5. We saw two _____ fishing for food.

Harcourt

Name _____

▶ **Write the word that completes each sentence. Read the story when you are finished.**

sorry   gone

_____

1. I am _____ I forgot our snack.

---

while   together

_____

2. We get hungry _____ we fish.

Bears   Once

_____

3. _____ we are home,
we will eat fish.

---

sound   bears

_____

4. The _____ will eat fish, too!

TRY THIS Write a sentence for the word <u>together</u>. Then draw a picture to go with your sentence.

SCHOOL-HOME CONNECTION Read this story together. Talk about food you like to eat and where it comes from.

Harcourt

▶ **Read the story. Circle the words that have the same vowel sound as in <u>mine</u>. Then write each word on the chart.**

Bear's Find

Bear sees a bee hive in a pine tree. He will go up the side of the tree. In a little while he will have lunch. The sweet treat will be fine. We like this lunch, but the bees are not nice.

1. _____	2. _____
3. _____	4. _____
5. _____	6. _____
7. _____	

TRY THIS Put all the <u>i-e</u> words in alphabetical order.

Name _____

▶ **Read the questions. Circle the answers.**

1. What is six plus three?

   time   nine

2. What sometimes has two wheels?

   bike   like

3. What do you do on a bus or in a car?

   ride   nine

4. What do you want to know when you look
   at a clock?

   bike   time

5. How do you feel about a friend?

   ride   like

TRY THIS Draw a picture for one of the spelling words.
Write the word under your picture.

SCHOOL-HOME CONNECTION Ask your child to write each
word he or she circled. Then circle the pair of rhyming words.

Welcome Home
Lesson 17   49

Harcourt

Name _____

► **Think about the story. Then fill in the story chart.**

Title of the Story	The Main Characters

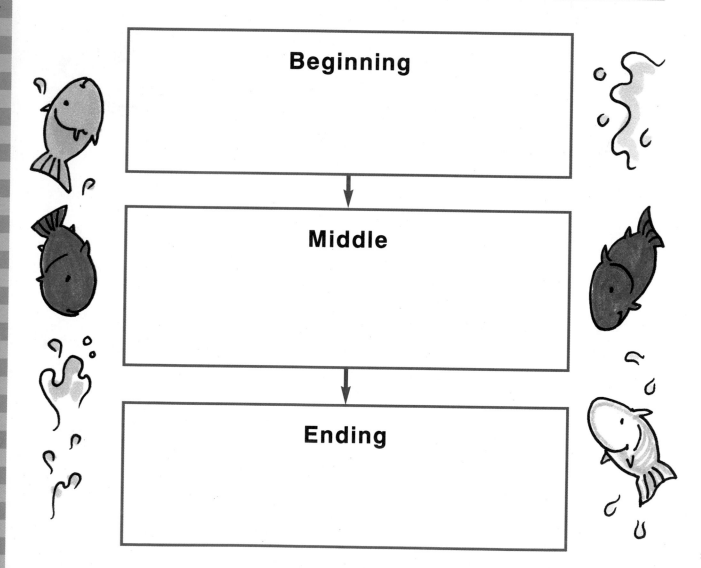

Beginning

Middle

Ending

TRY THIS Change the ending of the story. Write a new ending and draw a picture about it.

SCHOOL-HOME CONNECTION Ask your child to tell the story of Sam and Nelly. Talk about hibernation and the animals that hibernate.

Harcourt

▶ **Read the poem. Circle all the words that have the /ā/ sound spelled *a-e*. Write the words on the chart.**

I play in a wave,

I hide in a cave.

I race and play

A game all day.

I make my bed.

I'm always fed.

I take time to rest.

My home is the best!

_____	_____
_____	_____
_____	_____

TRY THIS Pick two words. Use them to write one sentence.
Draw a line under each word you use.

SCHOOL-HOME CONNECTION Read the words on the chart. Talk about the letter pattern CVC*e*. Think of other words with this pattern and write them on your own chart.

Welcome Home
Lesson 18   51

Harcourt

Name _____

▶ **Draw a picture to show what happens next. Write a sentence about your picture.**

1. _____

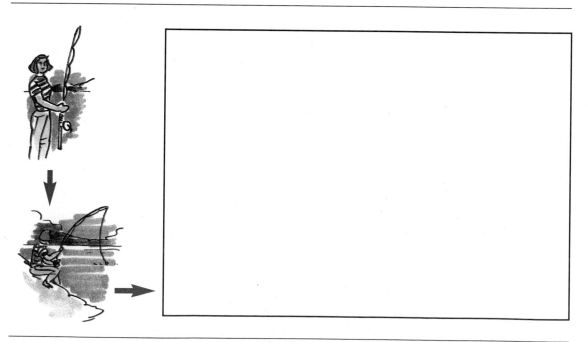

2. _____

SCHOOL-HOME CONNECTION Ask your child to tell you each story. Read aloud his or her sentence.

Harcourt

Name _____

▶ **Read the sentences. Write the word that matches each letter shape and makes sense.**

| When | wheels | whale | Where | Why |

1. ⬚⬚⬚⬚⬚ are you going?

2. ⬚⬚⬚ does the ⬚⬚⬚⬚

have ⬚⬚⬚⬚⬚⬚ ?

3. ⬚⬚⬚⬚ I race, this will go fast.

TRY THIS Draw two real things that have wheels. Write a sentence about each picture.

 SCHOOL-HOME CONNECTION Talk with your child about whales. Together, write a whale fact and draw a picture to go with it.

Harcourt

Name _____

► Write the word from the box that names each picture.

| bike | lake | cake | rake |

1. _____

2. _____

3. _____

4. _____

TRY THIS Use the words to make two lists, one with -ake words and one with -ike words. Add two more words to each list.

SCHOOL-HOME CONNECTION Read the lists of words. Say each word, and ask your child to spell it aloud.

Harcourt

Name _____

▶ **Write the word that best completes each sentence.**

city	space	ice	mice	nice

_____

1. A _____ is a busy place.

2. Did the _____ melt yet?

3. I want to blast into _____.

4. I eat fish. What do _____ eat?

5. My friends are _____.

TRY THIS Fold a piece of paper into four squares. Use four words from the box. Write one word on each square and draw a picture about each word.

SCHOOL-HOME CONNECTION Write the word *space*. Talk about the sound that *s* and *c* stand for. Circle all the letters on the page that sound like *s*.

Welcome Home
Lesson 21
55

Harcourt

Name _____

▶ **Read the ad. Then follow the directions.**

1. Find two color words. Color each.

2. Find two words that tell about size. Put a line under each.

3. Find a word that tells about shape. Circle it.

Fred's Fish Shop

Come to my big shop.

I have small fish for

your tank. Take home a

red fish or a yellow fish.

I have round fish. Fish are fun!

 TRY THIS Look around the classroom. Draw something you see. Write four describing words about it. Use words that tell about size, shape, and color.

SCHOOL-HOME CONNECTION Make a chart with three columns, one for color words, one for size words, and one for shape words. With your child, add words to each column.

Harcourt

Name _____

▶ **Read the clues. Then write the matching words in the crossword puzzle.**

| new ride pretty heard children school almost |

1.	Not quite.
2.	A place to study.
3.	Do this on a bus.
4.	Looks nice.
5.	Rhymes with <u>bird</u>.
6.	Means the same as <u>kids</u>.
7.	It's not old.

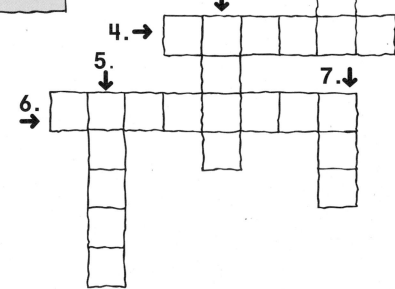

Harcourt

Name _____

▶ **Write the word that best completes each sentence.**

almost	ride	heard	School

1. We ⬜⬜⬜⬜ the bus.

2. ⬜⬜⬜⬜ is not far away.

3. He does not ⬜⬜⬜ .

4. He ⬜⬜⬜⬜ lost his hat.

 TRY THIS List all the vocabulary words that have an <u>o</u>. Make another list of all the vocabulary words with an <u>e</u>. Are any words on both lists?

SCHOOL-HOME CONNECTION Ask your child to write other sentences for the vocabulary words. Then ask him or her to read the sentences.

Harcourt

Name _____

► **Write the word that tells about the picture on the computer screen.**

whisper	whirl	wheel	when

1.

_____

- - - - - - - - - - - - - - -

_____

2.

_____

- - - - - - - - - - - - - - -

_____

3.

_____

- - - - - - - - - - - - - - -

_____

4.

_____

- - - - - - - - - - - - - - -

_____

TRY THIS Use each word in a sentence. Write the sentences.

Harcourt

SCHOOL-HOME CONNECTION Use four small cards. With your child, write one word on each card. On the other side of the card, write a riddle for the word. Share your riddles with a friend.

Name _____

▶ **Write the word from the box that best
matches the clue.**

| race | face | dance | mice | nice |

1. It's fun to hear the song
   and move to the beat.

_____

2. This can be happy or sad.

_____

3. Someone kind and good.

_____

4. A chance to test your
   skill.

_____

5. Small animals with
   long tails.

_____

SCHOOL-HOME CONNECTION Write each spelling word on a card.
Match the rhyming words. Then spell them aloud.

Harcourt

Name _____

▶ **Think about the story. Write your answers in the box.**

Things Cecil Can Do

▶ **Finish the sentence.**

_____

- - - - - - - - - - - - - - - - -

Cecil is best at _____

_____

- - - - - - - - - - - - - - - - -

_____

SCHOOL-HOME CONNECTION Ask your child to tell you about the story. Talk about real machines that help you at home.

Welcome Home
Lesson 22 **61**

Harcourt

Name _____

▶ **Look at the pictures and draw what happens next. Then write a sentence about your picture.**

_____

_ _

_____

_____

_ _

_____

SCHOOL-HOME CONNECTION Make up a three-part story. Tell the first two parts and have your child complete the third part. Repeat with a second story.

Harcourt

Name _____

▶ **Help the children line up in ABC order by their first names. Write their names in ABC order.**

Todd   Russ   Dan   Jenny

1. _____   2. _____

3. _____   4. _____

▶ **Line up the children's robots in ABC order. Write their names in ABC order.**

Wiz   Buzz   Zap   Fizz

1. _____   2. _____

3. _____   4. _____

Harcourt

SCHOOL-HOME CONNECTION Write all eight names on small cards. With your child, put all the names in ABC order.

Name _____

▶ **Circle the word that names the picture.
Write the word.**

1. face
space

_____

2. rice
mice

_____

3. space
trace

_____

4. mice
rice

_____

5. trace
space

_____

TRY THIS Cut out five squares. Write a clue for each word on the square. Write the answer word on the back. Give your clues to a friend to guess.

SCHOOL-HOME CONNECTION Ask your child to find three words on the page that rhyme. Think of other words that rhyme with them.

Harcourt

Name _____

▶ **Read the chart. Then write the contraction that completes each sentence.**

She is	She's
he is	he's
do not	don't
can not	can't
I will	I'll

1. Kate is tired. _____ going to bed.

2. The robot can move, but it _____ eat.

3. I want some cake. _____ make it.

4. Jack is late, but _____ coming.

5. I _____ have a red hat.

 SCHOOL-HOME CONNECTION Read the sentences with your child. Discuss item number 1. Ask your child to identify who is meant by the word *she's*. Discuss the word *he's* in number four.

Harcourt

Name _____

▶ **Read each sentence. Look at the red words in each sentence. Write the word that means the opposite of the red word.**

rest	last	best	must	fast

_____

1. My robot won **first** place. _____

_____

2. When is the weather **worst** ? _____

_____

3. Some people **work** outside. _____

_____

4. Some robots are **slow**. _____

_____

5. You **do not have to** march. _____

SCHOOL-HOME CONNECTION Use the words in the box. Pick a word and have your child use it in a sentence. Repeat for all the words.

Harcourt

▶ **Draw a picture to go with each sentence.**

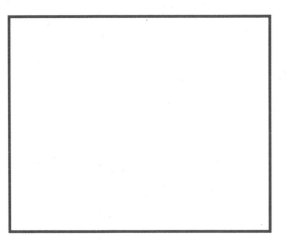

The clown has a purple wig.

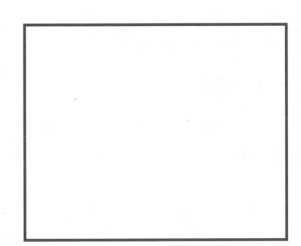

This clown has a frown.

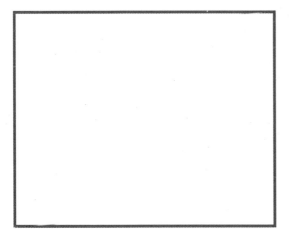

This clown has a crown.

A clown has a brown umbrella.

 TRY THIS Read each sentence again. Circle all the words that rhyme with <u>down</u>.

SCHOOL-HOME CONNECTION Draw a picture with your child of a brown cow downtown. Write a sentence to go with the picture.

Harcourt

Name _____

▶ **Read the chart. Write the word in the box that best completes each sentence.**

Taste words	Smell words	Sound words	Feel words
sweet sour	fresh moldy	loud quiet	cold hot

1.   is _____.

2. A  is _____.

3. A  is _____.

4. Hot  smells _____.

5. A  is _____.

SCHOOL-HOME CONNECTION Add one more word to each category in the chart on this page. Think of something that represents the new describing word.

Harcourt

▶ **Cut out the clue cards and the word cards. Put a word where it best finishes each sentence clue. Paste a word on each side of the clue cards.**

With five cents, I will ☐ gum.

Apples and plums are ☐.

Toad ☐ because he was happy.

In my fluffy coat, I am ☐.

The U.S. flag is red, white, and ☐.

Pumpkins are the color ☐.

In the fall, the leaves turn many ☐.

| buy | fruit | smiled | warm | blue | orange | colors |
| buy | colors | smiled | warm | blue | orange | colors |

Harcourt

Name _____

Pink and
purple are
☐ .

I am not
cold. I am
☐ .

I did not
frown. I
☐ .

He buys an
apple and an
☐ .

Dad's car
is dark
☐ .

What would
you like to
☐ ?

The quilt
has many
☐
in it.

Harcourt

Name _____

▶ **Read the story. Circle all the words
with <u>ow</u>. Write all of the words on the chart.**

Owl liked the barn. His home was up. Cow liked the
barn. His home was down. "How are you?" asked Owl.
"Right now I am hungry," said Cow. "Let's go to town."
So they went off in a brown car.

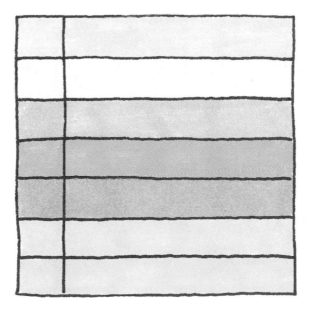

 TRY THIS Number the words to put them in ABC order.

 SCHOOL-HOME CONNECTION With your child, write a four-line
rhyme about Cow and Owl. Use the words from the chart to make
the rhymes.

Harcourt

Name _____

▶ **Use the words from the box to complete the story.**

| how | now | town | brown | down |

Toad went high up and looked

_____

_____. He saw green grass

_____

and _____ dirt. He went all over

_____   _____

_____. Toad knows _____

to stop. But he does not want to land right

_____

_____. He's having so

much fun!

SCHOOL-HOME CONNECTION Help your child use the words to write a story about a day he or she would like to spend with Toad.

Name _____

▶ **Think about the story. Then fill in the story map.**

Beginning

Middle

Ending

SCHOOL-HOME CONNECTION Ask your child to tell you about
The Absent-Minded Toad. Ask him or her if they think the title is a good
one, and why or why not.

▶ **Choose the word that best completes each sentence. Write the word.**

price	drive	hike	ride	hide

_____

1. I could _____ my bike.

_____

2. Where did I _____ it?

_____

3. I could _____ the car.

_____

4. What is the _____ for a cab?

_____

5. So, I'll just _____ to town!

SCHOOL-HOME CONNECTION Use the words to write a story together about two toads who are friends.

Harcourt

Name _____

▶ **Read Toad's shopping list. Circle all
the words with the same vowel sound as <u>team</u>.**

Shopping List

green apples
three oranges
one can pea soup
lean beef
ice cream
baked beans
tea bags
meatballs
milk

 TRY THIS Count the number of words you circled. Write the
number on the shopping list.

SCHOOL-HOME CONNECTION Make a three-column chart with
your child. Sort the *ee* and *ea* words in the list.

Welcome Home
Lesson 29   75

Name _____

▶ **Toad went to a silly market. Follow the directions.**

1. Color the green beans pink.

2. Color the corn many colors.

3. Color the carrots purple.

4. Color three tomatoes red and two orange.

5. Color the lettuce white.

6. Color the potatoes green.

SCHOOL-HOME CONNECTION Have your child give you directions for a simple task. Discuss the directions you received.

Name _____

▶ **Finish each ad by writing the word that best completes each sentence.**

| place | Lace | face | price |

_____

- - - - - - - - - - - - - - - -

_____

your shoes with neat colors.

See your

_____

- - - - - - - - - - - - - - - -

_____

here!

No one beats our

_____

- - - - - - - - - - - - - - - -

_____ for

rugs!

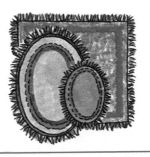

Mama's is the best

_____

- - - - - - - - - - - - - - - -

_____ for

pizza!

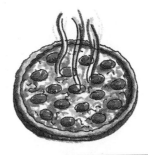

Harcourt

SCHOOL-HOME CONNECTION Ask your child to read each word in the box. Say each word and ask him or her to spell it aloud.

Name _____

▶ **Read the story. Write the word that best completes the sentence.**

sky	cry	fly	Why	try	tie

_____   _____

1. "_____ do you _____?"

Toad asked.

_____

2. "Because I can't _____ to my nest," said Owl.

_____

3. "I need to get up in the _____, but I can't

_____

get my _____ out."

_____

4. "I will _____ to help,"

said Toad.

SCHOOL-HOME CONNECTION Use the words to write a four-line rhyme about the story.

Harcourt

Name _____

▶ **Read the sentences. Each sentence tells how many. Circle the word that tells how many. Then color how many Frog bought.**

1. Frog got three lamps.

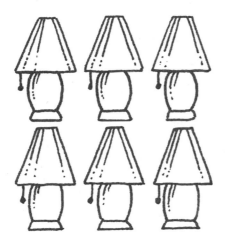

2. Frog picked five umbrellas.

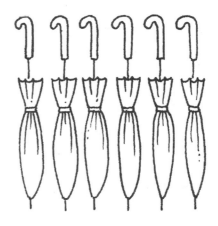

3. He got two plants.

4. He got one tent.

Harcourt

SCHOOL-HOME CONNECTION Ask your child how many plants and lamps Frog bought altogether. Help him or her write an addition sentence that tells how many.

Welcome Home
Lesson 31   79

Name _____

▶ **Read the story. Write the word that best finishes each sentence.**

| great | took | heads | might | water |

My Camping Trip

Mom and I went camping. We _____

sleeping bags and a tent. We put the boat in the

_____ . We found a _____ place to

put the tent. With hats on our _____, we went

for a hike. "We _____ go fishing," said Mom.

Name _____

cook	food	great	fire

_____   _____

Later we made a _____ to _____ the

_____

soup. We were hungry. We ate all the _____.

_____

We slept in the tent. It was a _____ camping
trip!

TRY THIS Write all the words that have five letters. Write a new story with these words.

SCHOOL-HOME CONNECTION Play a game. Write each vocabulary word on a small card. Mix the cards, and pick two. Say a sentence using both of the words.

Welcome Home
Lesson 32   **81**

Harcourt

Name _____

▶ **Write the word in the box that best completes each sentence.**

pie	cry	by	lie	try

_____

1. Toad and Owl sit _____ the fire.

_____

2. "Let's eat some _____," said Toad.

_____

3. Owl starts to _____.

_____

4. "I can't tell a _____," said Owl.

   "I ate the pie!"

_____

5. "Don't cry! I'll _____

   to cook some soup.

Welcome Home
Lesson 32

SCHOOL-HOME CONNECTION Work with your child to write three sentences using the word *by*.

Harcourt

Name _____

▶ **Read the story and circle all the
spelling words.**

I can not jump over the moon.
I can not get up in the sky. My
little dog does not laugh. My cat
does not play a song. My friends
know cows do not fly. They do not
wonder why. But they do ask me
how I make the best apple pie.

pie   my
why   sky
fly

▶ **Write the spelling words in ABC order.**

1. _____

2. _____

3. _____

4. _____

5. _____

SCHOOL-HOME CONNECTION Ask your child to write
some words that end with *y* and *ie*. Together, write a story
with the words.

Harcourt

Name _____

▶ **Think about the story. Then complete
the story chart.**

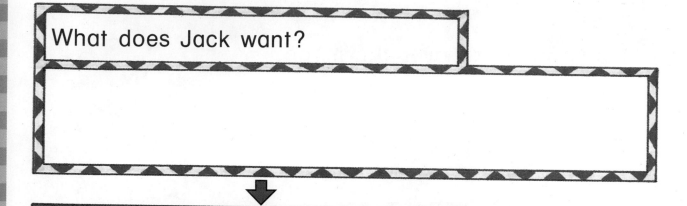

What does Jack want?

What does Jack do?

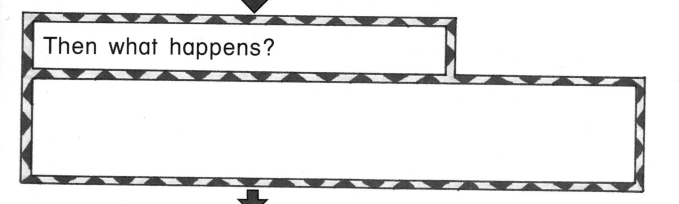

Then what happens?

How does the story end?

SCHOOL-HOME CONNECTION Ask your child to tell you
about *Tumbleweed Stew*. Discuss the ending. Brainstorm ideas
for Jack Rabbit's cactus pie.

Harcourt

Name _____

▶ **Use the words in the box to complete each asking or telling sentence.**

Where	Why	Who	When	What	while

1. _____ is hungry?

2. _____ is there to eat?

3. _____ will Mother come?

4. _____ can't we eat now?

5. _____ is Mother?

6. "We were hungry _____ you were away!"

SCHOOL-HOME CONNECTION Write each asking word on a small card. Take turns picking one card and using the word to ask a question.

Harcourt

▶ **Read about armadillos. Then write a sentence to answer each question.**

Armadillos are animals with very hard skin. They are the size of a cat. They have short legs, but they move fast. They eat worms, bugs, and snails. They roll up in a hard ball to keep safe.

1. How big are armadillos?

_____

- -

_____

2. What is their skin like?

_____

- -

_____

3. How do they keep safe?

_____

- -

_____

SCHOOL-HOME CONNECTION Talk or read about an unusual animal with your child. Draw a detailed picture together.

Harcourt

Name _____

▶ **Look at the picture. Do what the**
sentences say.

1. Color the snake red and blue.

2. Draw another owl next to this one.

3. Color the mice brown.

4. Color a plant green.

SCHOOL-HOME CONNECTION Give your child a
piece of paper and a crayon. Give him or her
simple directions to create a simple drawing.

Welcome Home
Lesson 34   **87**

Harcourt

Name _____

► **Use a contraction to complete each sentence.**

| don't | can't | doesn't | Jack's | He's | He'll |

1. _____ making a garden.

2. _____ growing potatoes.

3. He _____ want animals to eat the plants.

4. _____ make a gate so they _____ get in.

5. The animals _____ like it!

SCHOOL-HOME CONNECTION Review the contractions. Talk about the two words that make up each contraction.

Harcourt

▶ **Write the word that best completes each sentence in the story.**

home	nose	hole	stove	bone	mole

_____

1. This is a _____ in the dirt.

2. It is the door to my _____.

3. You see, I am a _____.

4. I sniff with my _____.

5. I have a _____.

6. I will make soup with this _____.

SCHOOL-HOME CONNECTION Use the phonograms -ole and
-one to form more words with long vowel o.

Welcome Home
Lesson 36   89

Harcourt

Name _____

▶ **Read the chart. Then write the word
that best finishes each sentence.**

| sunny | rainy | snowy | stormy | cloudy |

1. It is a _____ day.

2. It is a _____ day.

3. It is a _____ day.

4. It is a _____ day.

TRY THIS

Write a story about today's weather.

SCHOOL-HOME CONNECTION Together, read the weather
report in a newspaper. Help your child find words that
describe the weather.

Harcourt

► **Cut out the word cards. Read the clues in the boxes. Paste each word card below the matching clue.**

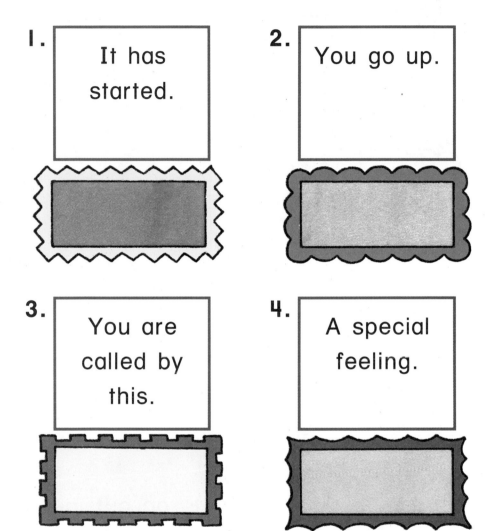

1. It has started.

2. You go up.

3. You are called by this.

4. A special feeling.

began	climb	love	name
began	climb	love	name

SCHOOL-HOME CONNECTION Three of the vocabulary words contain long vowels. (*began, climb, name*) Help your child listen for the long vowel sounds as you read the words together.

Harcourt

▶ **Use the word cards to finish each sentence. Paste the word card.**

5. My  is Carl.

6. I ⬜ up the steps.

7. It ⬜ to rain.

8. I would  to go outside.

Harcourt

Name _____

▶ **Read the sentences about Little Bear.**
Write the word that best completes each sentence.

alone	nose	those	home	close

_____

1. Little Bear has a little black _____.

_____

2. From the top of the tree he saw his _____.

_____

3. He can't fly like _____ birds.

_____

4. The little girl was lost and _____.

_____

5. I think they will be _____ friends.

TRY THIS Use this letter pattern: ☐ o ☐ e
Write four new words that fit the pattern.

SCHOOL-HOME CONNECTION Take turns with
your child using each word in a new sentence.

Welcome Home
Lesson 37   **93**

Harcourt

Name _____

▶ **Write the word in the box that best matches the clue.**

bone	home	joke	nose	note

_____

- - - - - - - - - - - - - - -

1. It lets us smell things. _____

_____

- - - - - - - - - - - - - - -

2. We laugh when we hear a silly one. _____

3. We do not eat this part, but dogs like it.

_____

- - - - - - - - - - - - - - -

_____

4. This is where you and your family live.

_____

- - - - - - - - - - - - - - -

_____

_____

- - - - - - - - - - - - - - -

5. You can read and write one. _____

TRY THIS Read the spelling words. Where do you hear the vowel sound? Color the box. | beginning | middle | end |

SCHOOL-HOME CONNECTION Write the words in one column. Have your child color in the *o*'s red, and trace the *e*'s in red. Talk about the pattern.

Harcourt

Name _____

▶ **Draw and write about what happens in
the beginning, the middle, and the end of
the story.**

Beginning

Middle

Ending

SCHOOL-HOME CONNECTION Have your child read his or her
sentences to you. Ask your child to tell you what could happen
in the next chapter.

Welcome Home
Lesson 37   95

Harcourt

Name _____

▶ **Read the story. Circle all the words with the same vowel sound as <u>cone</u>.**

Bear rode to see his friend Mole, but Mole was not home. Bear left a note for Mole. "Go to the flag pole at the park. We can jump rope." Bear rode to the park. There was Mole and some other friends too!

▶ **Write the words you circled.**

_____

- -

_____

- -

_____

SCHOOL-HOME CONNECTION Use the list of long *o* words to write a new story. Use Raccoon and Skunk in the story.

Harcourt

Name _____

▶ **Read about a bear. Circle the word that best completes each sentence. Write the word.**

The White Bear

This bear lives on ice and snow. He is white but has a black nose. When he hides his nose, he is all white. It is hard to spot him on the snow. He hunts birds, rabbits, and seals. He is the biggest of all bears.

white
blue
black

1. This bear is white but has

   _____

   a _____ nose.

rabbits
bears
plants

2. He hunts _____.

sea
beach
snow

3. He is hard to see in the _____.

oldest
biggest
smallest

4. He is the _____ of all.

SCHOOL-HOME CONNECTION Talk with your child about pets. Ask him/her to draw a picture of your pet or a friend's pet. Revisit the picture and together add details.

Welcome Home
Lesson 38

97

Harcourt

Name _____

▶ **Tess and Dan are at the ABC Zoo. The animals are in ABC order at this zoo. Write the names of the animals Tess and Dan see as they walk through the ABC Zoo.**

kangaroo	cheetah	hippo
tiger	ostrich	duck

1. _____

2. _____

3. _____   4. _____

5. _____

6. _____

Welcome Home
Lesson 39

SCHOOL-HOME CONNECTION Cut out 10 small cards. Make one card for each of the six animals at the ABC Zoo. Make four new cards: *ant*, *worm*, *pelican*, *rabbit*. Mix the cards and play a game. Pick one card and begin an ABC list. Take turns picking a card and adding it in the right ABC place.

Harcourt

Name _____

▶ **Add -ed or -ing to the word to complete each sentence. Remember to double the last letter before adding the ending.**

hop + ing

_____

- - - - - - - - - - - - - - - - - - - -

1. Rabbit was _____
through the grass.

stop + ed

_____

- - - - - - - - - - - - - - - - - - - -

2. She _____ to pick flowers.

skip + ing

_____

- - - - - - - - - - - - - - - - - - - -

3. She began _____ home.

hug + ed

_____

- - - - - - - - - - - - - - - - - - - -

4. Mother _____ her.

TRY THIS Make a list of each word with the -ed and the -ing ending. Write a new story using some of these words. Circle the words in your story.

 SCHOOL-HOME CONNECTION Ask your child to write the words *clap, wag, mop,* and *hum* on paper. Then write each word with the *-ed* and *-ing* endings.

Harcourt

Name _____

► **Use the words in the box to complete the sentences. Then read the story again.**

those	woke	nose	rose	poke

_____

1. "Did you _____ me?" asked Father.

2. "I did," said Bear, "with my little black

_____

_____."

3. "You _____ me up."

4. Bear gave Father a _____.

5. "I was just dreaming about _____!"

6. "My _____ knows!"

SCHOOL-HOME CONNECTION Make a list of the words in the box. Ask your child to sort them into two lists (-oke, -ose). Add two new words to each list.

Harcourt

Patch's Treat

This cat has black feet that look like socks.

Fold

Fold

Patch! Let's go home. You need a treat. I'll feed you.

8

Please, can I keep him? I'll try to keep my room neat.

6

2

Jean needs to find good homes for her cats.

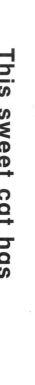

What should we call him?

7

---Fold--- ---Fold---

4

This sweet cat has a patch on his eye.

Please, can I keep him? He'll sleep in a small bed in my room.

5

Baseball!

✂

— Fold —

— Fold —

People like
to watch the
players step
up to the plate
and hit the ball.
CRACK!

✂

8

Children in many
countries play the game.

They play in the same way—

6 with a ball, a bat, and a mitt.

4

The game was
first played
in the United
States of America.
It was first called
"town ball." Later it
became baseball.

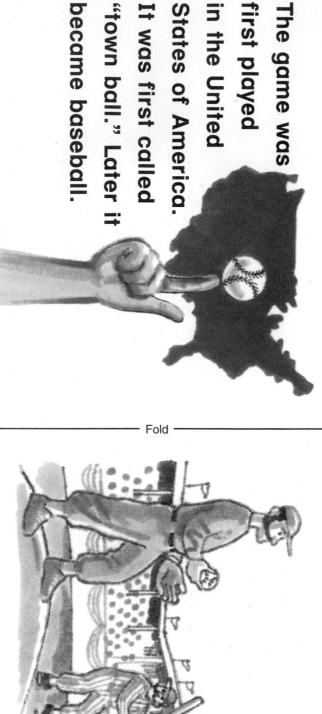

2

Baseball is played all over the
world. It doesn't take much to play
the game. You need a ball, a bat,
some mitts, and a big place to play.

5

7

A Piece of Cake

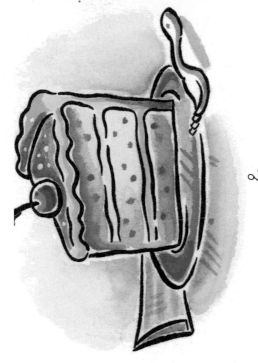

1

--- Fold ---

Oh, yes, that would be nice.
Do you have Sticky Cake?

3

--- Fold ---

This is just like the Silly Cake

8 my Mommy makes!

Aaah! I thought of a cake you

6 must try. We baked it this morning.

Would you like a piece of cake with your tea?

Here is a piece of Silly Cake.
Please tell me how you like it. 7

Too bad. Do you have
Happy Cake? Or even
Hungry Cake?

Sticky Cake?
No, we do not have Sticky Cake.

5

Once in a While

Fold

Fold

Once in a while, four white birds smile when they wonder about the one with the wide smile.

8

The one with the wide smile wondered and watched.

9

Five white birds shared the same nest. They ate together. They slept together.

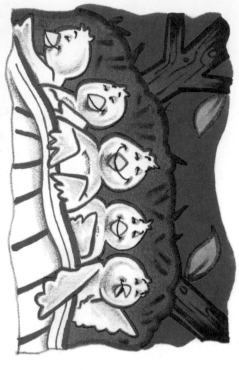

One day, the bird with the wide smile went on his way.

Once in a while, the one with the wide smile talked about going away.

4

Once in a while, the others laughed and said he was kidding. 5

How to Make a Face

— Fold —

Harcourt

✂

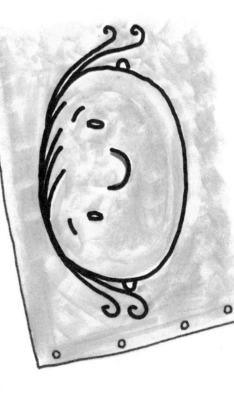

Make a nice big circle.

— Fold —

Harcourt

Now you make a pretty face yourself.

8

✂

You're almost finished. Make it look pretty. You can make your face fancy or simple.

9

4

In the center, make a nose.

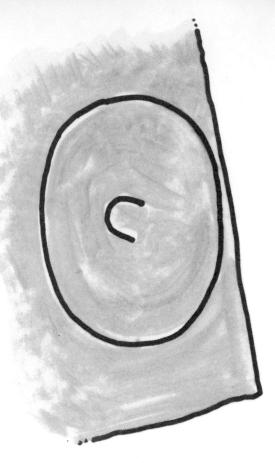

2

First use a pencil.

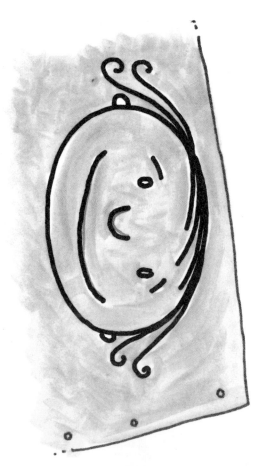

Fold

Fold

Don't forget the eyes.

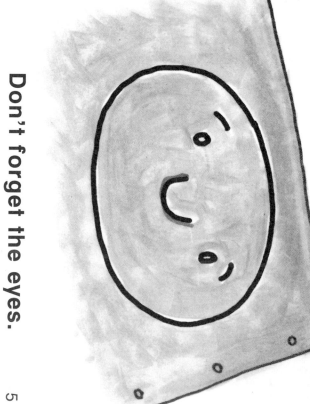

5

7

Brown Bear's Lunch

1

— Fold —

3

— Fold —

Brown Bear went back to town.

He got the things on his list

8 and flowers for his friend.

They talked and walked until

Brown Bear was home again.

He forgot about his list, but

6 he didn't forget about his lunch!

Brown Bear made a
list of things to buy.

Fold

He went to town and met a friend.
"How are you?" he asked. Brown
Bear and his friend talked and
walked and talked.

Fold

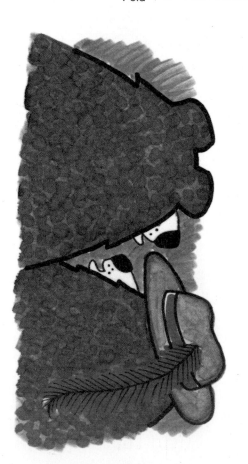

5

7

A Dream to Fly

1

"Some day I'll go up in the sky. I want to try."

3

--- Fold ---

I LOVE TO FLY

If you look in the sky, you might see Mike way up high.

8

--- Fold ---

Well, Mike got his wish. He got in a plane.

6

4

Mike went to school.
He wasn't shy.

2

Mike had a dream.
He wanted to fly.

"I'm going to fly. It's my dream to go up in the sky."

5

"It's as easy as pie!
Look, I can fly!"

7

Squirrels

Fold — Fold

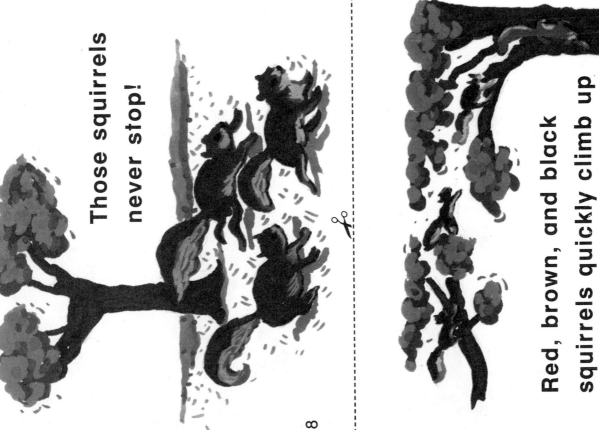

Those squirrels never stop!

8

Red, brown, and black squirrels quickly climb up trees and poles. Have you ever seen a squirrel hop from branch to branch?

6

Squirrels can be found
all over the world.
Some squirrels
build homes
in trees.

2

—✂—

— Fold —

Squirrels like to
dig holes for their
winter food. Their
sharp teeth help
them crack open
nuts and seeds.

4

— Fold —

—✂—

7

5

Set
Sail

▶ **Say each word. Circle the pictures that have the same vowel sound as <u>sight</u>. Then write the word.**

high	fright	night	sigh	light

1.

_____

- - - - - - - - - - - -

_____

2.

_____

- - - - - - - - - - - -

_____

3.

_____

- - - - - - - - - - - -

_____

4.

_____

- - - - - - - - - - - -

_____

5.

_____

- - - - - - - - - - - -

_____

6.

_____

- - - - - - - - - - - -

_____

SCHOOL-HOME CONNECTION Ask your child to show you the completed page. Let your child explain the answers he or she did not pick.

Harcourt

Name _____

▶ **Add <u>er</u> or <u>est</u> to the word so that it correctly completes the sentence. Write the word on the line.**

bright

_____

- -

1. This bird has _____

colors than that bird.

---

high

_____

- -

2. The blue bird lands on a _____

branch than the green bird.

---

tight

_____

- -

3. Birds make nests in the _____

places.

TRY THIS With a partner, act out the words <u>light</u>, <u>lighter</u>, <u>lightest</u> and <u>high</u>, <u>higher</u>, <u>highest</u>.

SCHOOL-HOME CONNECTION Have your child read you the completed page, and show you how he or she chose the answers.

Set Sail
Lesson 1

3

Harcourt

Name _____

▶ **Look at the blue bird's pictures. Write the word that best completes each sentence.**

joined   afraid

_____

- - - - - - - - - - - - - - - - - -

1. I was _____ to fly.

learn   flew

_____

- - - - - - - - - - - - - - - - - -

2. I will _____ how to fly.

afraid   flew

_____

- - - - - - - - - - - - - - - - - -

3. Mom _____ away.

afraid   joined

_____

- - - - - - - - - - - - - - - - - -

4. A little green bird _____ me for a walk.

Harcourt

joined   afraid

_____

- -

5. I was not _____ to fly any more.

flew   afraid

_____

- -

6. I _____ for a long time.

joined   afraid

_____

- -

7. I _____ another bird.

learn   flew

_____

- -

8. I think it is fun to _____ how to fly.

TRY THIS Make a drawing that shows how to help someone try a new thing. Write a sentence to go with the picture.

SCHOOL-HOME CONNECTION Read the completed page with your child. Write or say two rhyming sentences with the words *flew* and *grew*.

Set Sail
Lesson 2   5

Harcourt

▶ **Circle the words that have the same vowel sound as <u>might</u>.**

1. branch 	**2.** light 
3. night 	**4.** high 
5. fright 	**6.** nest 

 TRY THIS Write another word that rhymes with <u>sight</u>. Draw a picture for it.

SCHOOL-HOME CONNECTION Ask your child to show you the completed page. Let them explain the words he or she did *not* pick.

Harcourt

▶ **Write the word that best completes each sentence.**

| might | high | light | night | right |

_____

1. Birds fly _____ in the sky.

2. Do birds fly by day or

   _____

   at _____?

   _____

3. A bird _____ make its nest in a

   tree.

   _____

4. One nest is _____ here in this tree.

   _____

5. The eggs get heat and _____

   from the sun.

SCHOOL-HOME CONNECTION Ask your child to read you the completed page. Then make a list of more words that rhyme with *high* or *light* and have the letters *igh*.

Set Sail
Lesson 2

7

Name _____

▶ **Think about the story. Then complete
the flowchart.**

The blue bird is afraid to fly.

He looks for nothing.

 TRY THIS Write a new ending for the story you read.

8 Set Sail
Lesson 2

SCHOOL-HOME CONNECTION Think of a story you both
know. Retell it to each other.

Harcourt

Name _____

▶ **Read the paragraph. Write the main idea in the box. Write the details in the circles.**

Ducks are born knowing many things. Ducklings know that they must follow their mother. Ducklings also know how to swim. The mother does not have to show them.

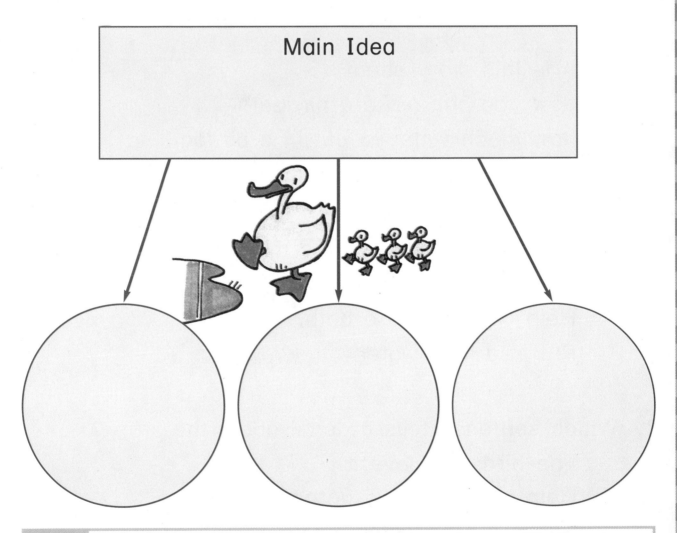

Main Idea

TRY THIS Think of a pet or other animal you know. Find out what things that animal knows when it is born. Find out what things the animal has to learn.

SCHOOL-HOME CONNECTION Ask your child to read the paragraph at the top of this page to you. Together, think of a title for the paragraph.

Set Sail
Lesson 3   9

Harcourt

▶ **Read the story. Then choose the best answer. Fill in the oval in front of the best answer.**

Bird Baths

Help a bird have a bath. Put a plastic pan outside. A table is a good spot. Put in a little water. Don't make it too deep. The birds will love it.

1. What is this story about?
   - ⬯ how you can make a birdbath
   - ⬯ how much water to put in a birdbath
   - ⬯ why you should use a plastic pan

2. What sentence tells you the main idea?
   - ⬯ The birds will love it.
   - ⬯ Help a bird have a bath.
   - ⬯ Put in a little water.

3. Which sentence tells a detail about the story?
   - ⬯ The birds will love it.
   - ⬯ Help a bird have a bath.
   - ⬯ Put in a little water.

SCHOOL-HOME CONNECTION Tell your child that this page is to help them learn how to fill out a special kind of answer form that they will use at times while they are in school.

Harcourt

Name _____

► **Choose the word that completes the sentence. Write it on the line.**

perch   port   porch
_____

- - - - - - - - - - - - - - -

1. A large bird landed on my _____ .

corn   cork   cake
_____

- - - - - - - - - - - - - - -

2. I gave it some _____ to eat.

shirt   short   sport
_____

- - - - - - - - - - - - - - -

3. It stayed only a _____ time.

storm   torn   stork
_____

- - - - - - - - - - - - - - -

4. It was a _____ .

short   sort   porch
_____

- - - - - - - - - - - - - - -

5. I have never seen that _____ of bird.

SCHOOL-HOME CONNECTION Have your child find the word *stork* on the page.

Set Sail
Lesson 4   **11**

Harcourt

Name _____

▶ **Read each sentence. Write the word that completes the sentence. Remember to drop the _e_.**

surprise   +   ed
_____
- -

1. The bird was _____ .

taste   +   ed
_____
- -

2. She _____ blueberries.

chase   +   ing
_____
- -

3. "No one is _____ me," she said.

believe   +   ed
_____
- -

4. "I never _____ I could fly."

TRY THIS Add _-ed_ or _-ing_ to the words <u>taste</u>, <u>like</u>, and <u>bake</u>. Write a sentence for each new word.

SCHOOL-HOME CONNECTION Ask your child to read you the completed page. Add _-ing_ to answer words that end with _-ed_, and make new sentences with those words.

Harcourt

Name _____

▶ **Circle the word that names the picture. Then write the word.**

1.

hat   hot   hay

_____

- - - - - - - - - - - - - -

_____

2.

pan   play   paint

_____

- - - - - - - - - - - - - -

_____

3.

rain   ride   rail

_____

- - - - - - - - - - - - - -

_____

4.

snack   sail   snail

_____

- - - - - - - - - - - - - -

_____

5.

tray   tail   trap

_____

- - - - - - - - - - - - - -

_____

6.

tree   tired   train

_____

- - - - - - - - - - - - - -

_____

TRY THIS Write a word that rhymes with <u>hay</u> and has <u>ay</u>. Write a word that rhymes with <u>snail</u> and has <u>ai</u>. Draw a picture for each word.

SCHOOL-HOME CONNECTION Ask your child to share the finished page with you. Together, make up a sentence for each answer.

Harcourt

Name _____

▶ **Look at the picture. Write a verb to complete each sentence.**

| play | stay | wait | mail |

_____

1. Frog wanted Toad to _____ ball.

_____

2. Toad wanted to _____ a letter first.

_____

3. Frog said, "I will sit and _____ for you."

_____

4. Toad asked Frog to _____ for supper.

TRY THIS Work with a partner. Make a list of as many verbs as you can.

SCHOOL-HOME CONNECTION With your child, look for some other verbs on this page. (*asked, said, sit, wanted*)

Harcourt

Name _____

▶ **Cut out the cards and play a matching game. Match each word with the sentence it completes.**

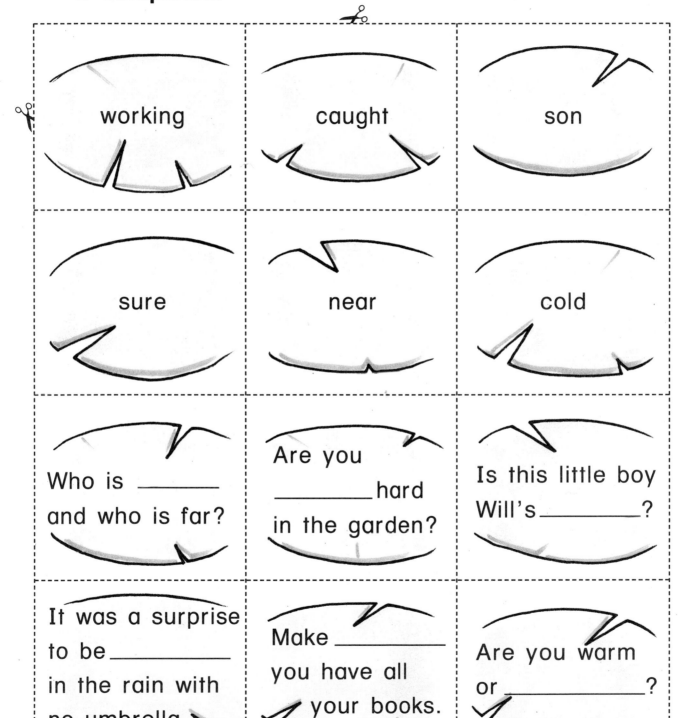

working

caught

son

sure

near

cold

Who is _____ and who is far?

Are you _____ hard in the garden?

Is this little boy Will's _____?

It was a surprise to be _____ in the rain with no umbrella.

Make _____ you have all your books.

Are you warm or _____?

Harcourt

SCHOOL-HOME CONNECTION Work with your child to create sentences that include the vocabulary words.

Set Sail
Lesson 7 **15**

Name _____

Harcourt

Name _____

▶ **Look at the picture. Then write the word from the box that completes each sentence.**

play	stay	day	rain	wait

_____

1. I do not like the _____ .

_____

2. I can't _____ outside.

_____

3. I don't want to _____ home.

_____

4. I want a sunny _____ .

_____

5. I will _____

for the sun to come out.

TRY THIS Use the words <u>mail</u>, <u>day</u>, and <u>gray</u> to write a short poem or story about the weather.

SCHOOL-HOME CONNECTION Ask your child to read you the completed page. Together, make up a few sentences about what the toad did after the sun came out. Use words with *ai* and *ay*.

Set Sail
Lesson 7   **17**

Harcourt

Name _____

▶ **Write the word that best completes each sentence. Circle the <u>ay</u> or <u>ai</u> in the words that you write.**

day	rain	may	tail	play

1. Ray, can you come out and _____?

2. It is a sunny, warm spring _____.

3. What did you say? You _____?

4. Do you think it will _____?

5. The puppy chases after

_____

its _____.

SCHOOL-HOME CONNECTION Have your child show you the different ways long *a* is spelled.

Harcourt

Name _____

► **Frog hears that spring is just around the corner. Color the blocks that tell where Frog goes in the story.**

kissed his mother	walked down a path	
walked into a cave	walked in the meadow	
walked on big stones	walked along the river	walked in a field of corn
swam at the beach	went around his house	jumped in the lake

► **How do you know when it is spring?**

_____

_____

_____

_____

SCHOOL-HOME CONNECTION Discuss with your child how the phrase "spring is just around the corner" means spring is coming soon.

Set Sail
Lesson 7   **19**

Harcourt

► **Read the story to find out where the snail went. Draw his trail. Then circle all of the words that have the same vowel sound as <u>may</u>.**

Snail's Rainy Day

Rainy days made Snail happy. He played on the steps, and then he came down. Snail played in the pail, but liked playing with paint the most. He played on the drain. He played under the mailbox. At the bay, Snail saw a ship with a sail. He got on and sailed away.

TRY THIS Use the words <u>sail</u>, <u>train</u>, and <u>main</u> to tell more about what the snail did after he got on the ship.

SCHOOL-HOME CONNECTION Read the story aloud. Have your child clap each time you read a word with long vowel a.

Harcourt

Name _____

▶ **Read the word above each line. Add
-ed or -ing to the word to complete the
sentence. Remember to drop the e.**

like
_____
- - - - - - - - - - - - - - - - - -

1. I have always _____ spring.

rake
_____
- - - - - - - - - - - - - - - - - -

2. My dad is _____ the leaves.

chase
_____
- - - - - - - - - - - - - - - - - -

3. I do not like _____ snowflakes.

make
_____
- - - - - - - - - - - - - - - - - -

4. Are you _____ a snowman?

bake
_____
- - - - - - - - - - - - - - - - - -

5. We _____ cookies.

SCHOOL-HOME CONNECTION Read the completed
page with your child. Discuss your favorite seasons.
Use words with -ed and -ing.

Set Sail
Lesson 10   **21**

Harcourt

Name _____

► **Choose the words that best complete the sentence. Write the words on the lines.**

mail **main**	1. What is the _____ _____ thing you like about _____?	
pail **pain**	2. Jake was in _____ when he tripped over the _____.	
trail **train**	3. The _____ went past an old forest _____.	

TRY THIS List as many words as you can that rhyme with <u>main</u> or <u>mail</u>. Give yourself one minute.

22 Set Sail Lesson 10

SCHOOL-HOME CONNECTION Ask your child to show you the completed page. If necessary, help him or her complete the page.

▶ **Choose a word in the box that rhymes
with each underlined word and makes sense.
Write it on the line.**

find	behind	wild

1. Do you <u>mind</u>? There's a large

_____

- - - - - - - - - - - - - - - - - -

frog _____ us.

---

2. At the zoo, a <u>child</u> read a sign. It said,

_____

- - - - - - - - - - - - - - - - - -

"Do not feed our _____ animals."

---

3. You need to <u>wind</u> this toy.

_____

- - - - - - - - - - - - - - - - - -

The baby will _____

it and play with it.

TRY THIS Make your own pair of sentences with two words
from the box or other words that rhyme with them.

SCHOOL-HOME CONNECTION Discuss the finished page with your
child. Help him or her notice the *i* sound in each word.

Set Sail
Lesson 11   **23**

Harcourt

Name _____

▶ **Write the verb that best completes each sentence.**

drink	find	help	make	fill

_____

1. I _____ the birdbath.

2. Birds _____ from it.

3. They come and _____ seeds in our feeder.

4. We _____ birds because we like them.

5. I _____ bird feeders for my friends.

TRY THIS Work with a friend to read a news story about a sports team. Together, find the verbs that tell about now.

SCHOOL-HOME CONNECTION Have your child read you the completed page. Together, make up some more sentences that use the verbs from this page.

Harcourt

Name _____

▶ **Read each sentence. Cut out the words at the bottom of the page. Paste the words in the correct place to finish each sentence.**

1. I like to [   ] to the rain.

2. Do you [   ] for puddles?

3. Of [   ] I do.

4. Rainy days are [   ] .

5. What was the [   ] puddle you ever saw?

6. You [   ] me about that.

listen   told   different

care   largest   course

SCHOOL-HOME CONNECTION Check that your child has pasted the words in the correct place. Review the vocabulary words and their meanings.

Set Sail
Lesson 12   25

Harcourt

Name _____

Set Sail
Lesson 12

Harcourt

Name _____

▶ **Choose the word from the box to best complete each sentence.**

| find | behind | wild | blind | mind |

1. It can see.

_____

- -

It is not _____.

2. It is not tame.

_____

- -

It is _____.

3. It is not lost.

_____

- -

I can _____ it.

4. A tadpole's tail is not in front.

_____

- -

It is _____.

5. A tadpole doesn't think like we do.

_____

- -

It has a _____ of its own.

SCHOOL-HOME CONNECTION Ask your child to show you the finished page. Together use the sentences to make up a definition for each word in the box.

Name _____

▶ **Circle the words in the puzzle. Then use them to answer the questions.**

child	kind	wild	find	mild

s	o	w	i	l	d	k	n	d
s	i	n	g	c	h	i	l	d
m	i	l	d	n	a	n	e	s
a	c	x	f	i	n	d	o	p

1. This _____ plays in the rain.

2. It is a soft, _____ rain.

3. He jumps like a _____ animal.

4. What _____ of animal is he?

5. I will _____ out!

SCHOOL-HOME CONNECTION Ask your child to tell you how the words *child*, *wild*, and *mild* are the same, and how they are different.

Name _____

▶ **Think about the story. Then fill in the story map.**

1. What does the boy's mother say?	2. What is the boy's first problem?

3. How is this problem solved?	4. What problem does the boy face next?

5. How does the elephant solve this problem?	6. What happens at the end of the story?

TRY THIS Circle the parts of the story map that you think could really happen.

SCHOOL–HOME CONNECTION Read this page together with your child. Discuss problems and solutions in daily activities.

Set Sail
Lesson 12 **29**

Harcourt

Name _____

▶ **Read each sentence. Write <u>real</u> or
<u>not real</u> on the lines.**

1. He can sail a boat.   _____

2. The cat can sail a boat.   _____

3. Fish need raincoats.   _____

4. Rain makes puddles.   _____

5. He can think about a cat.   _____

 TRY THIS Pick one of the sentences that tells about something
not real. Draw a picture of it. Write <u>not real</u> under it.

SCHOOL-HOME CONNECTION Have your child share the completed
page. Together, list some other things that are *real* or *not real*.

Harcourt

Name _____

▶ **Write the word from the box that best completes each sentence.**

| large | age | bridge | edge |

_____

1. I came to a _____ puddle.

2. An alligator sat by the

_____

_____ of the puddle.

3. I wanted a _____ so

I could get over the puddle.

_____

4. Kids my _____ like puddles.

TRY THIS Make a chart about the ages of your classmates. Give your chart a title that uses the word <u>age</u>.

SCHOOL-HOME CONNECTION Ask your child to read you the finished page. Together, think of as many words as you can that have the soft g sound.

Set Sail
Lesson 14
31

Harcourt

▶ **Look at the picture. Write the word to complete the sentence. Remember to double the last letter before you add ed or ing.**

step + ed

_____

1. Marco _____ outside.

slip + ing

_____

2. He began _____ and fell!

stop + ed

_____

3. Marco _____ to think.

snap + ed

_____

4. He _____ his fingers and went back inside.

step + ing

_____

5. Marco is _____ into his skates.

SCHOOL-HOME CONNECTION Ask your child to show you the completed page. Work together to write new sentences for the answer words.

Harcourt

Name _____

▶ **Read the numbered clues. Use the words from the box to complete the puzzle.**

hello	gold	no	also
ago	cold	soda	go

Across

2. a long time ___

3. ____ pop

4. stop and __

6. _____, how are you?

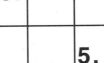

Down

1. icy ____

2. me ____ (too)

4. silver and ____

5. __, thanks

SCHOOL-HOME CONNECTION Ask your child to share the completed page. Then work together to list some words that rhyme with *old*, and to write some clues for these words. See if a friend can guess the words.

Harcourt

Name _____

▶ **Write <u>am</u>, <u>is</u>, or <u>are</u> to finish each sentence.**

_____
- - - - - - - - - - - - - - -

1. What _____ you doing?

_____
- - - - - - - - - - -

2. I _____ playing with a yo-yo.

_____
- - - - - - - - - - -

3. _____ you good at it?

_____
- - - - - - - - - - -

4. My sister _____ better.

_____
- - - - - - - - - - -

5. She _____ helping me.

_____
- - - - - - - - - - -

6. I _____ taking lessons from her.

 TRY THIS Work with a partner to answer the question "What are you doing?" Answer two ways—beginning with "I am" and with "We are."

SCHOOL-HOME CONNECTION Take turns with your child making up new sentences using *am*, *is*, and *are*.

► **Choose the word that best completes each sentence. Write it on the line.**

boy
buy
but

1. I need to find the _____.

and
air
at

2. Is he up in the _____?

both
buy
best

3. I can't see _____ near and far.

flew
few
five

4. Do you see a _____ boys down the street?

edge
egg
each

5. They are on the _____ of the puddle.

Harcourt

bought   brought

_____

- - - - - - - - - - - - - - -

6. I _____ my glasses.

edge   eggs

_____

- - - - - - - - - - - - - -

7. It scares me to look over the _____.

▶ **Look for the vocabulary words in this puzzle.**

1.	c	a	r	a	i	r	c	a	t
2.	t	h	b	r	o	u	g	h	t
3.	g	o	o	d	e	d	g	e	l
4.	b	o	t	h	m	e	m	i	t
5.	f	i	v	e	f	e	w	m	e

TRY THIS Make a list of the things a squirrel might want to find in a bed.

SCHOOL-HOME CONNECTION With children, review vocabulary words and their meanings.

Harcourt

Name _____

▶ **Choose the word that best completes each sentence. Write it on the line.**

fold   old   told

_____

- - - - - - - - - - - - - - - -

1. Mr. Rabbit is stuck in his _____ bed.

go   so   got

_____

- - - - - - - - - - - - - - - -

2. Mr. and Mrs. Rabbit _____ get a new bed.

soda   spot   sofa

_____

- - - - - - - - - - - - - - - -

3. Mr. Rabbit sees a nice _____.

Old   Sold   Socks

_____

- - - - - - - - - - - - - - - -

4. Mr. and Mrs. Rabbit say, "_____!"

TRY THIS Make up some rhyming sentences using the words <u>sold</u>, <u>old</u>, and <u>told</u>. Say your sentences to the class.

SCHOOL-HOME CONNECTION Have your child find the long *o* words that were not used as answers. Ask him or her to read them aloud and explain why they weren't the answers.

Set Sail
Lesson 17 **37**

Harcourt

Name _____

▶ **Write the word that best completes each sentence.**

both	go	old	no	Oh

_____

- - - - - - - - - - - - - - - - -

1. "_____!" said Bear.

_____

- - - - - - - - - - - - - - - - -

2. "My hat is so _____."

_____

- - - - - - - - - - - - - - - - -

3. "You have _____ hat at all."

_____

- - - - - - - - - - - - - - - - -

4. "We must _____ to the hat store."

_____

- - - - - - - - - - - - - - - - -

5. "We _____ will go."

SCHOOL-HOME CONNECTION Look over the answers your child wrote. Ask him or her to circle the letter *o* in each word.

Harcourt

Name _____

▶ **Think about how Poppleton shopped for a new bed. Fill in the web to show what he did.**

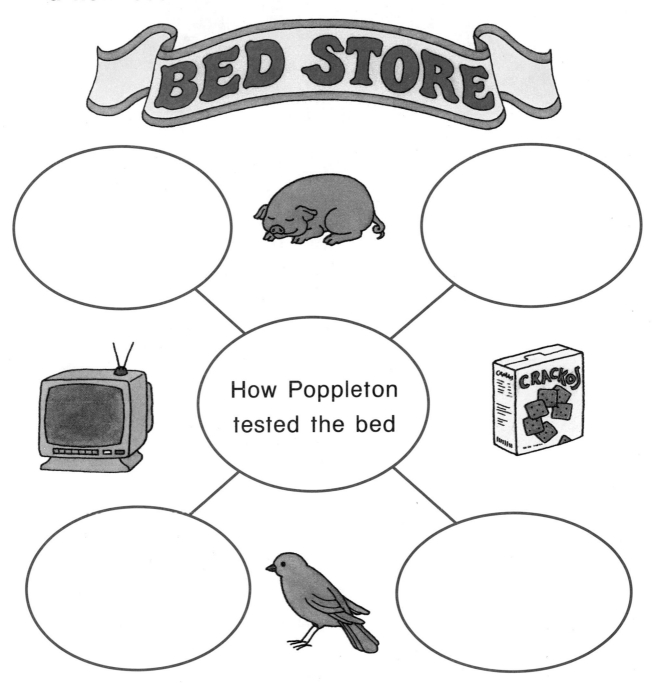

How Poppleton tested the bed

TRY THIS Think about your favorite place. Make a list of things you like to do there.

SCHOOL-HOME CONNECTION Read the finished page together with your child. Discuss how people make good choices about the things they buy.

Harcourt

▶ **Circle the sentence that tells about each picture.**

1. "Let's go!" said the colt.

"No!" said the girl.

"Hello!" said the ant.

---

2. A pig thinks he is cold.

A pig thinks he has lost his gold.

A pig thinks he has lost his tie.

---

3. I am opening the house now.

I am over on the sofa.

I am holding the gold in this safe.

4. I have a total of 3 bags.

I have a total of 3 cans.

I have a folded coat.

---

5. "Have no fear! Cold soda is here!"

"Have no fear! Your sofa is here!"

"Have no fear! Colt and the gold are here!"

---

6. The pig holds his gold.

The colt keeps the gold.

The colt calls the pig.

SCHOOL-HOME CONNECTION Review the completed page with your child. Then make up a new adventure for the superhero colt.

Harcourt

Name _____

▶ **Look at the picture. Then do what the sentences tell you to do**.

1. Make the pig on stage pink.

2. Give the pig a huge hat.

3. Find the largest bed. Put a badge on it.

4. Draw a huge pillow on one edge of the bed.

5. Find the cage next to the largest bed. Draw a pet gerbil inside the cage.

6. A large crowd is watching from the bridge. Draw a ring around the large crowd.

TRY THIS Write a sentence about this picture. Use some of the words from the sentences under the picture.

SCHOOL-HOME CONNECTION Go over the completed page with your child. Then have your child circle the words that contain the /j/ sound.

Harcourt

▶ **Finish each sentence. Write the contraction for the two words above each sentence.**

They've	You've	You'd	We'd	We're

We are

_____

- - - - - - - - - - - -

1. _____ in our new bed.

We would

_____

- - - - - - - - - - - -

2. _____ love you to come see.

You have

_____

- - - - - - - - - - - -

3. _____ been here before.

They have

_____

- - - - - - - - - - - -

4. _____ got their own bed.

TRY THIS Make a list of things you would like. Begin each item on your list with the words <u>I'd like</u>.

SCHOOL-HOME CONNECTION Ask your child to read the completed page aloud to you. Help your child use each contraction in a sentence.

Harcourt

Name _____

▶ **Add the ending <u>ed</u> and <u>ing</u> to each word. Remember to drop the final <u>e</u>.**

	ed	**ing**
close		
scare		
snore		

▶ **Write the correct word from the chart to finish each sentence.**

1. Why am I _____ this door?

2. The pig is _____ in his sleep.

SCHOOL-HOME CONNECTION Read your child's completed sentences aloud. Have him or her say "stop" each time you get to a word with an *-ed* or an *-ing* ending. If your child has difficulty identifying the ending by hearing it, have him or her point to the word on the page.

Harcourt

Name _____

▶ **Circle the word that best completes each sentence. Then write the word.**

1. "The moon is _____," said the cat.

hand
huge
tube

2. "It smells like _____," said the mule.

perfume
cute
perform

3. The cat sniffed but could not smell

_____

the _____.

purple
perfume
huge

4. "_____ me, but it has no smell," said the cat.

Every
Excuse
Cube

5. "Oh! _____ me!" said the mule. "I was sniffing the flowers."

Empty
Plume
Excuse

SCHOOL-HOME CONNECTION Ask your child to read the completed page to you. Then ask your child to explain in his or her own words what the story is about.

Harcourt

Name _____

▶ **Write the word that best completes
each sentence.**

spilled	filled	needed	cleaned

_____

1. Luke _____ to make ice cubes.

_____

2. He _____ the ice tray with water.

_____

3. The water _____ all over.

_____

4. Luke _____ up

the mess.

TRY THIS Take turns with a partner reading the sentences and
acting them out.

SCHOOL-HOME CONNECTION Have your child read the completed
page to you. Ask him or her to tell you what the words would be if
they were action words about the present time.

Harcourt

Name _____

▶ **Read each clue and look at the picture. Then write the clue word that best completes each sentence.**

appear	break	clear	idea	quietly

1. Don't yell or shout.

_____

_____

Be sure to talk _____ .

2. This starts inside your mind.

_____

_____

It's an _____ .

3. It's not there.

_____

_____

Can you make it _____ ?

4. The stars shine bright. The sky

_____

_____

is very _____ tonight.

Harcourt

5. Rabbit and Mole were tired.

_____

_ _ _ _ _ _ _ _ _ _ _ _ _ _ _ _ _

They took a _____ .

▶ **Look at the letters on the puzzle. Then write each vocabulary word where it fits on the puzzle.**

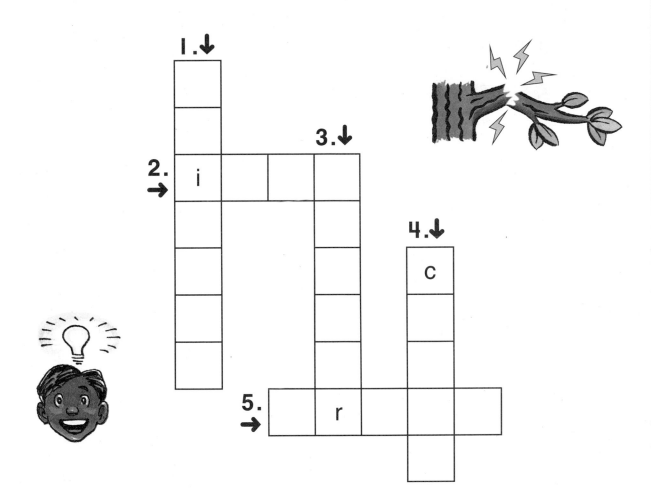

TRY THIS Make up your own clues and sentences for each word. See if a partner can answer them.

 SCHOOL-HOME CONNECTION Make clues for your child for each of the answer words on the page.

Set Sail
Lesson 22   47

Harcourt

▶ **Write the words in the box that will
finish the story.**

| cube | huge | Excuse | cute |

_____

- - - - - - - - - - - - -

"_____ me," said Mole. "I am never coming

_____

- - - - - - - - - - - - -

out! I am small, but I want to be _____.

_____

- - - - - - - - - - - - -

I want my den to be shaped like a _____."

_____

- - - - - - - - - - - - -

"Please come out! You are _____,"

Mule said. "You are my good friend, too."

SCHOOL-HOME CONNECTION Work with your child to write
original sentences for the words *cute, huge, cube,* and *excuse.*

Harcourt

Name _____

► **Write the word in the box that best completes each sentence.**

cute	use	rude	mule	cube

1. My _____ is on the moon.

2. Is the moon a _____?

3. Can you _____ your ears to hear the moon?

4. Is it _____ to stare at the moon?

5. Do you see a _____ face in the moon?

SCHOOL-HOME CONNECTION Ask your child which questions have answers that are true and which questions have a false answer. Ask your child to write a true sentence about the moon.

Harcourt

Name _____

▶ **Think about the story. Then fill in the
story map.**

Title:	**Characters:**
Moon Rope	

**What is the
first problem?**

How is it solved?

**What is the
second problem?**

How is it solved?

What do we learn about Fox and Mole?

SCHOOL-HOME CONNECTION Ask your child to retell the
story of *Moon Rope* with this completed page as a guide.

Harcourt

Name _____

▶ **Circle and write the word that best completes each sentence.**

night
noise   1. It happened late last _____.
new

built
bright   2. The sky was very _____.
brother

rolled
right   3. The birds flew _____ over us.
ready

should
sight   4. This _____ was a big surprise.
shout

mother
mixed   5. You _____ see it too.
might

SCHOOL-HOME CONNECTION With your child, recite the poem that begins "Star light, star bright." Ask your child to identify the words that end in *ight*. Write the words to the poem on paper and have your child circle the *ight* words

Harcourt

▶ **Write the word from the box that best completes each sentence.**

We've	You're	We're	I'd

_____

1. _____ here!

2. _____ been riding so long!

3. _____ like to take your bags.

4. _____ tired.

Come on in.

TRY THIS Write a poem about a day at the beach. Use words with 've, 'd, and 're.

Harcourt

Name _____

▶ **Circle the word that fits best in each sentence. Write it on the line to complete the sentence.**

hoping

hoped   1. I am _____ to get

host   something new.

placing

placed   2. I will be _____ it

place   in my yard.

Raked

Raking 3. _____ each fall will

Rake   not be hard.

tasting

taste   4. I have _____ the fruit.

tasted   Try some.

like

liked   5. I saw it and _____ it and

liking   planted it too.

SCHOOL-HOME CONNECTION Ask your child
to read the completed page to you. Have him
or her write the base word for *hoping*. (*hope*)

Set Sail
Lesson 23   **53**

Harcourt

▶ **Read the words in the box and look at the pictures. Then finish each postcard.**

| knee | remember | straight |

Dear Joey,

 Last night, Dad and I went out. We watched the moon come up. It seemed to come

_____

_____ up over the sea.

I found a big pink shell right next to my

_____ _____

------------------------ ------------------------------------

_____. I _____

that you like shells. When can you come over and see it?

 Your pal,

 Spencer

Dear Spencer,

    I was happy to get your card. The moon is full and

_____

shiny right now. I am glad you _____

that I like shells. When you get back, I'll come

_____

_____

_____ to your house. I want to

see this shell up close. It looks like it is as big

_____

_____

as your _____ !

            Your best buddy,

            Joey

Harcourt

SCHOOL-HOME CONNECTION Have your child choose one of the vocabulary words. Together, think of words that can be formed with the letters in the vocabulary word. Have your child write them and check.

Set Sail
Lesson 26

55

Name _____

▶ **Fill in the story frame to tell about the story. Draw a picture for each sentence.**

The Big Big Sea

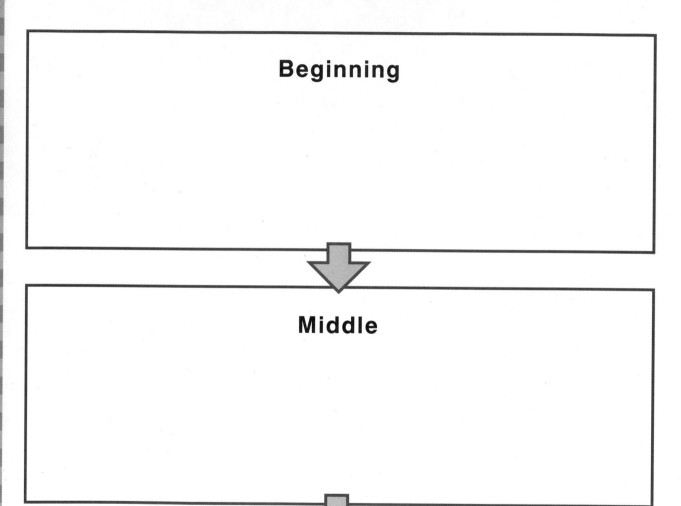

Beginning

Middle

End

SCHOOL-HOME CONNECTION Review a simple story you and your child know and discuss the beginning, the middle, and the end.

Harcourt

Name _____

▶ **Write <u>was</u> or <u>were</u> to complete each sentence. Then circle <u>one</u> or <u>more than one</u> to show how many people or things the action word tells about.**

one

1. I _____ skating all day.   **more than one**

one

2. They _____ skating, too.   **more than one**

one

3. We _____ in a pile!   **more than one**

one

4. We _____ all okay.   **more than one**

TRY THIS Together with a classmate, tell about three things that happened yesterday. Use <u>was</u> and <u>were</u> in your discussion.

🚌 **SCHOOL–HOME CONNECTION** Ask your child to read this page to you and explain his or her answers.

Harcourt

Name _____

► **Write the word that best completes each sentence.**

might	night	flight	light

_____

1. Look at the birds in _____ .

_____

2. We saw them last _____ , too.

_____

3. I can see by the _____ of the moon.

_____

4. They _____ come again.

TRY THIS Write these answer words as a list. Then list all the other words you can with <u>igh</u> that stand for the long <u>i</u> sound.

SCHOOL-HOME CONNECTION With your child, recite the poem that begins, "Star light, star bright." Ask your child to identify the words that end in *ight*. Write the words to the poem on paper so that your child can see as well as hear the *ight* words.

Harcourt

Name _____

▶ **Write the word from the box that best completes each sentence.**

feet	need	deep	sea	real

_____

1. I go with Mom to the _____.

_____

2. The water is not _____.

_____

3. I just got my _____ wet.

_____

4. I _____ my flip-flops, please.

_____

5. There is _____ salt in
the water.

SCHOOL-HOME CONNECTION Read the completed page
with your child. Make a list of the words that are spelled
with *ee* and a list of words spelled with *ea*.

Set Sail
Lesson 27   59

Harcourt

Name _____

▶ **Read the paragraph. Find the sentence that tells the main idea. Write it on the lines. Then write a title for the paragraph.**

Title

_____

- -

_____

Much more than water is in the sea. The sea is filled with living things. Many animals and plants live there. Some of the animals look like plants. We use many of the living things that are in the sea.

Main Idea

_____

- -

_____

- -

_____

- -

_____

Set Sail
Lesson 27

SCHOOL-HOME CONNECTION Read a picture book with your child. Discuss the main idea of the story.

Harcourt

Name _____

▶ **Write the word from the box that best completes each sentence.**

| day | rain | say | pail | gray | play |

_____

1. It is a sunny _____.

_____

2. What did you _____?

_____

3. I have my _____.

_____

4. My friend wants to _____.

_____

5. The sky turned _____.

_____

6. It's starting to _____.

SCHOOL-HOME CONNECTION Ask your child to read the finished page to you. Then work together to list more words that contain the long vowel a sound spelled ay or ai.

Harcourt

Set Sail
Lesson 29   **61**

▶ **Choose the word that finishes each sentence. Write it on the line.**

plan   planned   planning
_____

1. I had _____ to go to bed.

wagged   wag   wagging
_____

2. My dog was _____ his tail.

tapped   tap   tapping
_____

3. Who is _____ at the door?

hugging   hug   hugged
_____

4. I _____ my grandma at the door.

SCHOOL-HOME CONNECTION Ask your child to read the completed page to you. Together, write sentences for some of the answer words not used.

Name _____

▶ **Complete each contraction pair.**

1. I have

_____

- - - - - - - - - - - - - -

_____

2. They had

_____

- - - - - - - - - - - - - -

_____

3. You have

_____

- - - - - - - - - - - - - -

_____

4. You are

_____

- - - - - - - - - - - - - -

_____

5. We have

_____

- - - - - - - - - - - - - -

_____

6. We are

_____

- - - - - - - - - - - - - -

_____

 TRY THIS Write two sentences about things you can explore at the beach. Use two or more contractions in your sentences.

SCHOOL-HOME CONNECTION On index cards or small pieces of paper, write each word pair and each contraction. You and your child hold the cards like playing cards. Try to match word pairs and contractions. The player with the most pairs wins.

Harcourt

Name _____

▶ **Finish each sentence. Choose the
correct word that has the same vowel sound as
the underlined word. Circle the word and write it.**

feather
bread
meat

1. I <u>fed</u> the bird. I gave it some

_____

- - - - - - - - - - - - - - - - -

_____ .

meal
breakfast
breath

2. I like to <u>help</u>. Today I made

_____

- - - - - - - - - - - - - - - - -

_____ .

breakfast
heat
weather

3. I'll go with <u>them</u> even in bad

_____

- - - - - - - - - - - - - - - - -

_____ .

instead
real
head

4. I sleep in my <u>bed</u>.
My bird rests on the sand

_____

- - - - - - - - - - - - - - - - -

_____ .

SCHOOL-HOME CONNECTION Have your child
explain how he or she chose the answers.

Harcourt

Name _____

▶ **Write go or went to complete each sentence. Then circle now or in the past to show when each action took place.**

1. You and I can _____ to the zoo.

    now

    in the past

2. We _____ last month.

    now

    in the past

3. We can _____ again.

    now

    in the past

4. The baboons _____ from rock to rock last time.

    now

    in the past

TRY THIS Work with a partner to change the sentences. If it is in the past, make it tell about now. If it is about now, make it tell about something in the past. Use the words go and went.

SCHOOL-HOME CONNECTION Share the completed page with your child. If he or she is confused about the terms "now" and "in the past," substitute the terms "today" and "yesterday."

Harcourt

► **Fill in the words in the box to finish each sentence. Then do what the sentences tell you to do.**

| disappear | ground | across | mouth | shook |

1. The baboon likes to _____

   _____

   in the tall grass. Draw a circle around her.

2. A hippo is resting in the pond, not on the

   _____

   _____

   _____ . Color the hippo gray.

   _____

3. The crocodile walks _____ the

   mud. Color the mud black.

_____
- - - - - - - - - -

4. The gazelle opens her _____ for a drink. Color the water blue.

_____
- - - - - - - - - -

5. The bird _____ his wings to get the water off. Draw drops of water coming off the bird.

▶ **Find each word in the puzzle. Circle it. Words go across only.**

s	h	o	o	k	f	r	l	b	n
d	i	s	a	p	p	e	a	r	b
c	h	r	n	p	m	o	u	t	h
a	g	n	g	r	o	u	n	d	y
o	a	v	a	c	r	o	s	s	i

TRY THIS Write a newspaper headline for the animal picture on page 66. Use the words <u>disappear</u> and <u>across</u>.

SCHOOL-HOME CONNECTION Ask your child to share the completed pages with you. Discuss what he or she marked on the picture on page 66.

Set Sail
Lesson 32   67

Harcourt

Name _____

▶ **Read the sentences. Do what they tell you. Circle the words that have the same vowel sound as <u>bread</u>.**

What Is Up Ahead?

1. It has feathers. Color the feathers blue.

2. Its web is spread between the branches. Color it red.

3. It is heavy and has a huge head. Color it gray.

4. It looks like bad weather. Circle the storm clouds.

5. A crocodile is taking a bath. Color it green.

TRY THIS Make funny or scary warning signs. Each one should include the word <u>ahead</u>.

SCHOOL-HOME CONNECTION Share the completed page with your child. Find the words with the short *e* sound spelled *ea*. Work together to make up new sentences for those words.

Harcourt

Name _____

▶ **Read the words in the box. Then write the correct word in each sentence.**

| bread | Get | head | led | ready |

_____   _____

1. _____ the _____!

_____

2. We are _____.

_____

3. Watch your _____!

_____

4. Who _____ the ants here?

SCHOOL-HOME CONNECTION Read over the completed page with your child. Then help him or her think of more words with the short *e* sound in *head* or *get*.

Set Sail
Lesson 32 **69**

Harcourt

Name _____

▶ **Think about what Baboon learned about
the world. Then finish the web.**

The
world
is _____ .

SCHOOL-HOME CONNECTION Ask your child to read the answers
he or she wrote to complete the page. Discuss why Baboon gave
so many answers.

Harcourt

Name _____

▶ **Complete the sentences. Use the words in the box. Write each word on a line.**

arm	far	part	start	yard

_____
- - - - - - - - - - - - - - -

1. How _____ does the world go?

_____
- - - - - - - - - - - - - - -

2. You _____ right here.

_____
- - - - - - - - - - - - - - -

3. Stretch out your _____ .

_____
- - - - - - - - - - - - - - -

4. I can reach your _____ .

_____
- - - - - - - - - - - - - - -

5. That is the best _____ .

TRY THIS Where in the world would you like to go most? Write a sentence or draw a picture that tells about the place.

SCHOOL-HOME CONNECTION Ask your child to read you the completed page. Then have him or her use the words *far* and *yard* in sentences.

Set Sail
Lesson 33   **71**

Name _____

► **Read what Baboon says. Circle the pictures and words he is talking about.**

1.  These things are hot.

fire   steam   ice cream   sun

2.  These things are hard.

pillow   ice   bricks   wood

3.  These things are crunchy.

popcorn   toast   water   leaves

4.  These things are heavy.

bowling ball   feather   truck   hippo

TRY THIS Make a list of things you can find or think of that are light.

SCHOOL-HOME CONNECTION Share the completed page with your child. Ask him or her to think of more things that are heavy, crunchy, hard, or hot.

Harcourt

Name _____

► **Complete each sentence. Write the word on the line.**

JUNGLE REPORT — MAY 1st

spotting spotted spot

_____

- - - - - - - - - - - - - - - - - -

1. We have _____ a chimpanzee family.

patted pat patting

_____

- - - - - - - - - - - - - - - - - -

2. They are _____ and cleaning each other.

stepped stepping step

_____

- - - - - - - - - - - - - - - - - -

3. One baby chimp _____ right up to us.

patting pat patted

_____

- - - - - - - - - - - - - - - - - -

4. I _____ his hand.

nap napping napped

_____

- - - - - - - - - - - - - - - - - -

5. Now he is _____. What a find!

Harcourt

SCHOOL-HOME CONNECTION Take turns creating sentences using *-ed* and *-ing*. Discuss the different meanings of the sentences depending upon the tense.

Name _____

▶ **Write the word that best completes each sentence.**

| planet | spacecraft | rocket | space | pictures |

_____

1. I wonder what's in _____ .

_____

2. Saturn is a _____ with rings.

_____

3. The _____ lifted off the ground.

_____

4. Stars and planets are in _____ .

_____

5. The _____ flew to the satellite.

_____

6. The satellite takes _____ .

Set Sail
Lesson 36

Harcourt

▶ **Read the words in the box. Put them in the chart. You can use the words more than once.**

pictures	sun	stars	spacecraft	planet
moon	rocket		telescope	shuttle

Things in Space

Things We Can See from Earth

Ways to Travel in Space

Things That Help Us Learn About Space

SCHOOL-HOME CONNECTION Discuss space exploration during your lifetime with your child. Explain that rockets preceded the space shuttle program.

Set Sail
Lesson 36

Harcourt

▶ **Write the word on the line that best completes each sentence.**

| cold | So | ago | go | old |

1. The first trip to space took place over

   _____

   -

   40 years _____.

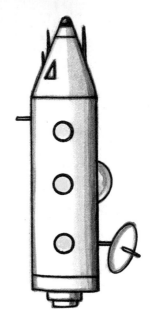

2. Space is very _____.

   _____

   -

3. Those who _____ up are brave.

   _____

   -

4. John Glenn was 77 years _____
   when he made his second trip.

USA

   _____

   -

5. _____ would you go if you could?

TRY THIS Pretend you are looking at Earth from space. Write a sentence describing what you see.

SCHOOL-HOME CONNECTION Ask your child to list other words that have the long *o* sound.

Harcourt

Name _____

▶ **Think about what you read. Fill in
the chart.**

Planets

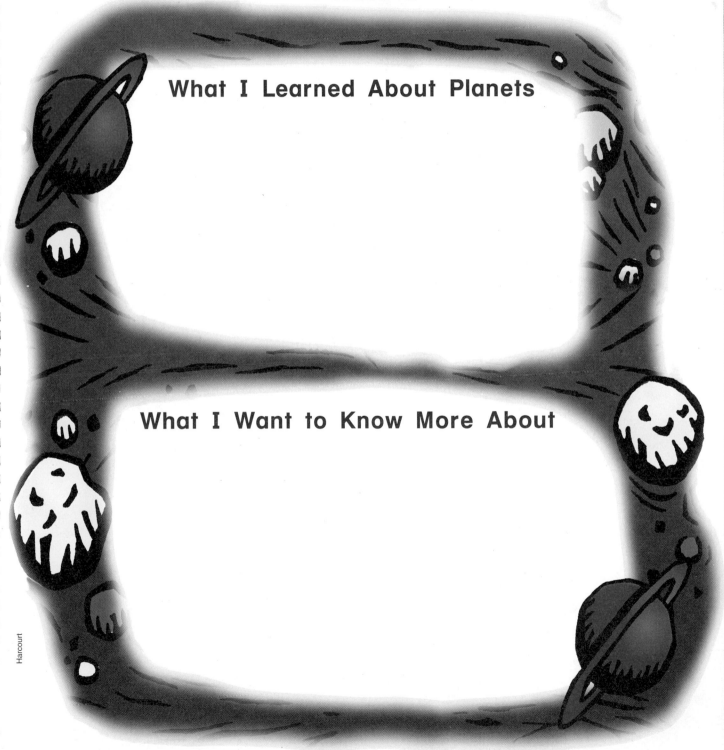

What I Learned About Planets

What I Want to Know More About

Harcourt

SCHOOL-HOME CONNECTION Ask your child to read you
the completed page. Ask him or her what fact was the most
interesting or surprising.

Set Sail
Lesson 36   77

Name _____

▶ **Write the word to finish each sentence.**

isn't   don't   hasn't
_____
- - - - - - - - - - - - - - - - - - - -

1. The spacecraft _____ landed yet.

aren't   isn't   don't
_____
- - - - - - - - - - - - - - - - - - - -

2. We _____ have long until we reach Mars.

3. Mars has two moons, but they

don't   isn't   aren't
_____
- - - - - - - - - - - - - - - - - - - -

_____ very big.

don't   hasn't   doesn't
_____
- - - - - - - - - - - - - - - - - - - -

4. Mars _____ have water.

 TRY THIS Make two lists. Call one list "Things I Like" and the other list "Things I Don't Like." Which list is longer?

🏠 **SCHOOL-HOME CONNECTION** Work with your child to think of sentences that use the words *doesn't* and *don't*.

Harcourt

Name _____

▶ **Write the word that best completes each line of the invitation.**

| bright | light | night | right | might |

A Star-Gazing Party!

Where: Cindy's house

_____

- - - - - - - - - - - - - - - -

When: Tuesday _____ at 8 o'clock.

_____

- - - - - - - - - - - - - - - -

Please bring a flash_____. Venus should

_____

- - - - - - - - - - - - - - - -

be _____ at sunset. If there are no

_____

- - - - - - - - - - - - - - - -

clouds, we _____ see Mars.

_____

- - - - - - - - - - - - - - - -

Please come _____ on time!

Cindy

555-1133

SCHOOL-HOME CONNECTION Play a game with your child. Write the word *right*. Under that word, write *bright*. Ask your child to tell you what letter you added. Repeat with the words *might*, *light*, *night*, and *sight*, asking your child to tell you what letter you changed.

Set Sail
Lesson 37 **79**

Harcourt

Name _____

▶ **Read the clues. Write the words to complete the puzzle.**

| cold | fold | most | roll | hold |

Across

3. do this with a ball

5. make something small and neat

Down

1. keep something in your hand

2. not hot

4. greatest amount

Set Sail
Lesson 37

SCHOOL-HOME CONNECTION Work with your child to write
a sentence for each of the Spelling Words.

Harcourt

Name _____

▶ **Read the paragraph. Circle the main idea and write four details about the paragraph on the rocks.**

In 1997, people learned a lot about Mars from a robot. A robot car called Rover traveled to Mars. The Rover's job was to collect facts about Mars. The Rover picked up rocks. It took pictures. It collected facts about the weather on Mars.

Things the Rover Did

TRY THIS Use the main idea to make up a title for the paragraph.

 SCHOOL-HOME CONNECTION Read newspaper captions with your child. Discuss photos and captions.

Set Sail
Lesson 37   **81**

Harcourt

► **Complete each sentence. Write the word on the lines.**

| huge | mule | cube | tune | use |

1. All planets are in the shape of a ball.

_____

- - - - - - - - - - - - - -

Not one is a _____.

2. Planets are very, very big.

_____

- - - - - - - - - - - - - -

Planets are _____.

3. So far, we see no life on other planets.

_____

- - - - - - - - - - - - - -

A _____ could not live on Pluto.

4. Spacecraft run on batteries.

_____

- - - - - - - - - - - - - -

These _____ the sun's light for power.

5. There is no air in space, so it is silent.

_____

- - - - - - - - - - - - - -

If you play a _____, no one will hear.

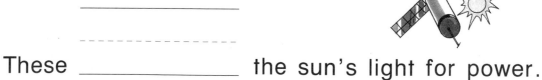

SCHOOL-HOME CONNECTION Ask your child to read to you the completed page. Discuss his or her answer choices.

Harcourt

Name _____

► **Circle the word that best completes each sentence. Write it on the line.**

small
smaller
smallest

1. Which planet _____

is the _____ of all?

smallest
small
smaller

2. The moon is _____

than Earth.

new
newest
newer

3. The _____ telescope is
called the Hubble Space Telescope.

oldest
old
older

4. Find out if this star is _____
than that star.

TRY THIS Draw a picture to show these words: long, longer, longest.

SCHOOL-HOME CONNECTION Use the words *big* and *small*
to compare the sizes of familiar objects in the home.

Set Sail
Lesson 40   **83**

Harcourt

▶ **Find these words in the puzzle. Circle them. The words go across and down.**

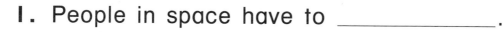

| eat | treat | heat | neat | meat |

g	r	o	w	e	a	t
m	e	a	t	c	a	r
a	v	a	n	e	m	e
h	e	a	t	b	y	a
b	a	g	n	e	a	t

▶ **Complete each sentence.**

1. People in space have to _____ .

2. They _____ special food.

3. Peanuts make a good _____ .

4. Still, it is hard to stay _____ .

5. Chicken and beef are two kinds of _____ .

SCHOOL-HOME CONNECTION Ask your child to show you how he or she solved the word-search puzzle at the top of the page.

Harcourt

The Long Flight

1

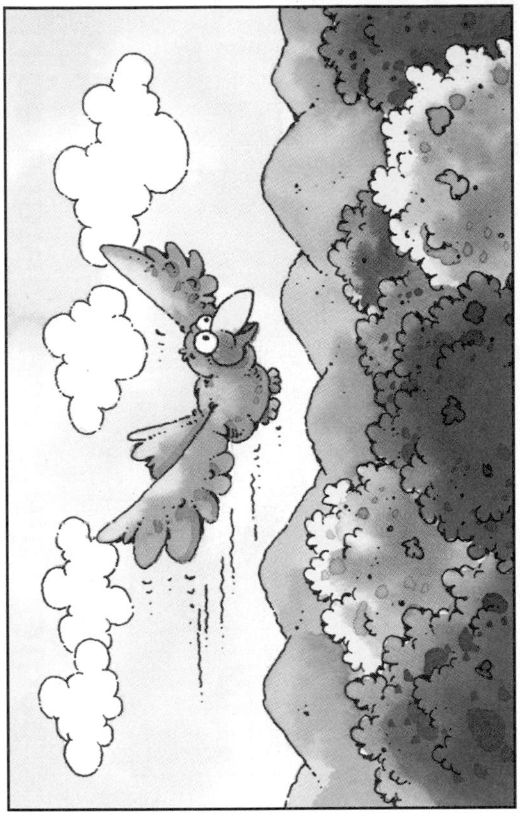

Fall came. Blue Bird flew higher and higher.

— Fold —

— Fold —

Blue Bird found a wonderful warm home.

8

Blue Bird flew a long time. The sky got lighter and lighter.

6

Blue Bird grew and grew.

The winter grew chilly. Other birds joined him as he flew.

The days got brighter and brighter.

Sometimes there was nothing to eat. Blue Bird was not afraid.

Fold

Fold

Frog and Mouse

1

— Fold —

3

Mouse could not stay and play. He had to work.

— Fold —

Then the two played near the woods.

8

"Make sure you get set for winter. Then you may play."

6

4

Winter was near. Mouse did
not want to be caught in the
cold without a home.

2

One gray night Frog wanted
to play with Mouse.

Fold

His father had said, "Always
find a winter home."

5

Frog helped Mouse until
the job was finished.

Home

7

88 Cut-out Fold-up Book

Find Something to Do

Fold

My tower crashes. My mom says, "Find something different to do."

Fold

How do you find something to do?

Of course I want to help.
This is something to do.

Set Sail
Cut-out Fold-up Book

89

2

On a rainy day my mom says,
"Find something to do."

7

We made the largest
cookies I've ever seen.

4

I run like a wild animal.
My mom says, "Listen child,
you need to mind."

5

"I need your help
with these cookies."

Crumbs in the Bed

— Fold —

"Do you want toast?" asked Jake.

— Fold —

Rover didn't stop. He ate both the jam and the toast. Now I have a bed full of crumbs!

Jake brought the toast. Rover had to see.

2

I am sick and in my bed.

— Fold —

Rover sniffed and jumped all over the bed. "Stop!" I shouted. 7

4

"Yes, cold toast with jam, please," I said.

— Fold —

Rover jumps on my bed. I told him to stop jumping.

5

Three Little Moles

1

Harcourt

"I'd be careful if I were you,"
he said. "On a clear day Snake
moves quietly in the grass."

3

— Fold —

Harcourt

— Fold —

Show the three moles
hiding in the hole.

8

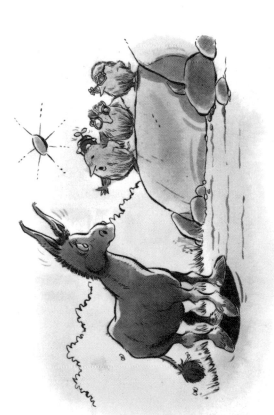

"You're rude, Mule,"
said the little moles.

6

"We are not afraid," the moles said.

An old mule spotted
three cute moles near
the edge of a hole.

— Fold —

— Fold —

The old mule said, "Snake can break
out fast. He looks like a long tube."

"I mean no harm to you. Go find
a safe place to hide," said Mule. 7

If I Went

to the Moon

1

— Fold —

If I could, I'd leave right now and fly straight there.

3

— Fold —

My home—the Earth.

8

When I got there, I'd put boots on my feet and take a walk. What would I see?

6

4

I'd sleep and eat in space.

2

It's not easy to go to the moon.

— Fold —

— Fold —

I'd read all about the moon.

5

7

THE RACE

— Fold —

3

The baboon led the way.

— Fold —

Who do you think will win?

THE RACE

8

The crocodile's head slipped under the water and disappeared.

6

Get ready. Get set. Go!

✂

The ostrich spread her feathers
and leaped into the race.

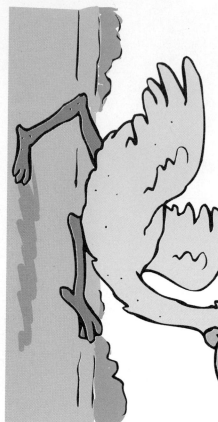

4

— Fold —

The gazelle is ahead now.

7

✂

The rhinoceros ran
across the meadow.

5

— Fold —

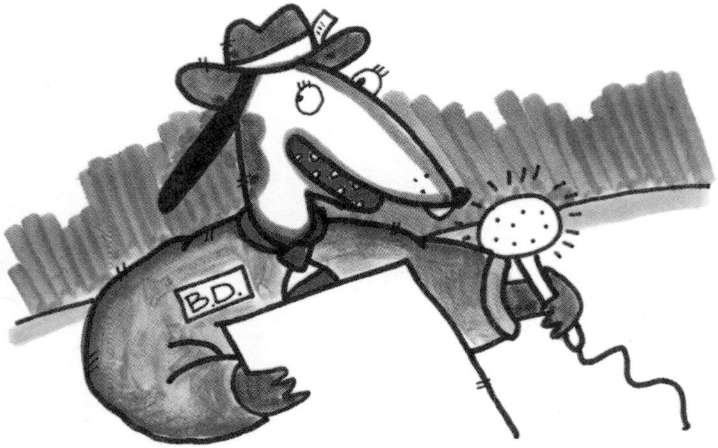

"There you have it. Two cats come home. So long from B.D. Reporter."

8

Harcourt

Fold

Cats in Space

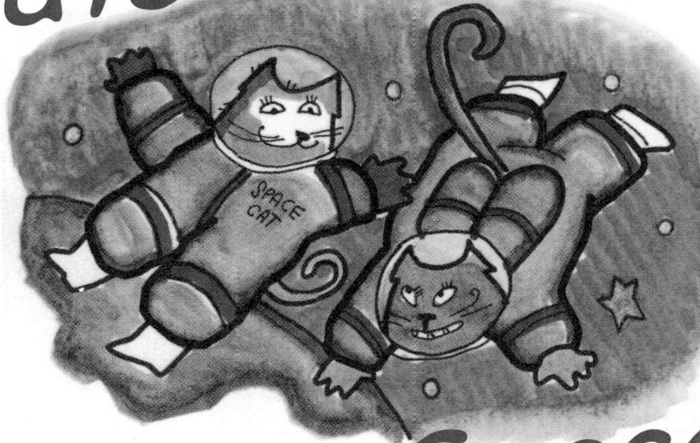

1

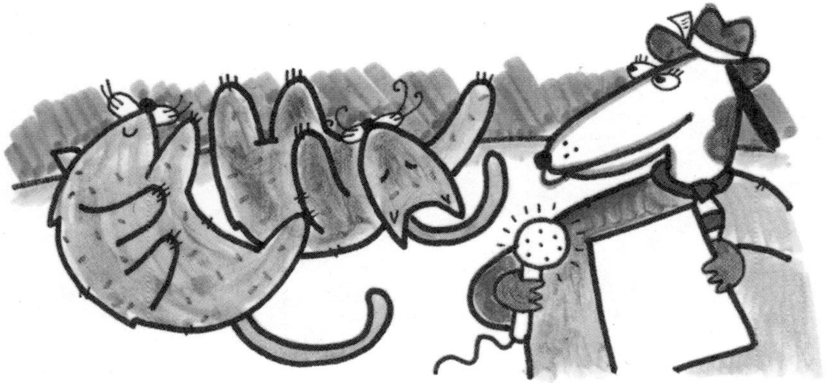

"Now that you are home, what do you want to do first?"

"We want to roll on the ground."

6

Fold

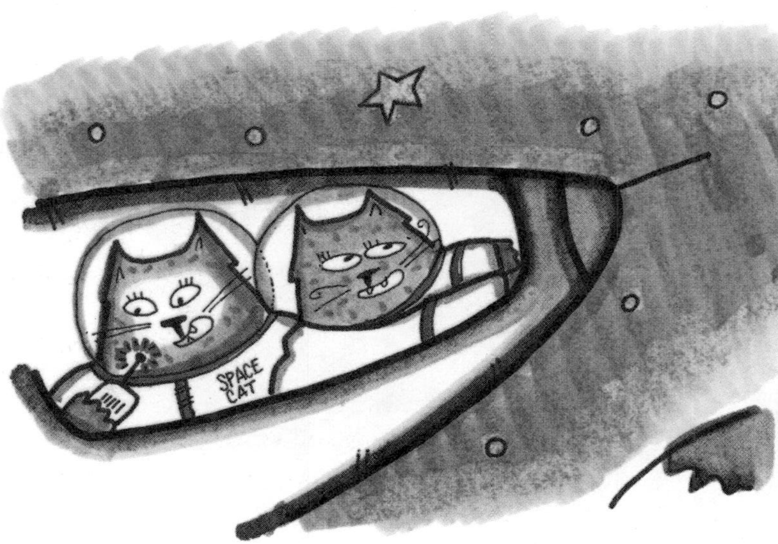

Harcourt

3

"It's very cold. I wouldn't go there again."

"Welcome home. What is it like on Pluto?"

"Hello. Two cats flew to Pluto in a rocket. In just a moment we will ask them about their trip to this cold planet."

Fold

Fold

Skills and Strategies Index

COMPREHENSION

Classifying **L5** 72
Main Idea **L4** 26 **L5** 9, 60, 81
Make Predictions **L4** 15, 52, 62
Noting Details **L4** 39, 86, 97
Practice Tests **L4** 16, 27, 40 **L5** 10

Reality and Fantasy **L5** 30
Retell and Summarize **L4** 14, 24, 37, 50, 61, 73, 84, 95 **L5** 8, 19, 29, 39, 50, 56, 70, 77

GRAMMAR

Contractions with *Not* **L5** 78
Describing Words: Color, Size, Shape **L4** 56
Describing Words: *-er, -est* **L5** 3
Describing Words: Feelings **L4** 45
Describing Words: How Many **L4** 79
Describing Words: Taste, Smell, Sound, Feel **L4** 68
Describing Words: Weather **L4** 90

Names of Holidays **L4** 9
Using *Am, Is,* and *Are* **L5** 34
Using *Go* and *Went* **L5** 65
Using *He, She, It,* and *They* **L4** 32
Using *I* and *Me* **L4** 19
Using *Was* and *Were* **L5** 57
Verbs **L5** 14
Verbs That Tell About Now **L5** 24
Verbs That Tell About the Past **L5** 45

PHONICS

Consonants
/j/*g, dge* **L5** 31, 41
/s/*c* **L4** 55, 60, 64

Contractions
's, n't, 'll **L4** 42, 65, 88
've, 'd, 're **L5** 42, 52, 63

Digraphs
/hw/*wh* **L4** 53, 59, 85

Inflections
-ed, -ing **L4** 99 **L5** 12, 21, 32, 43, 53, 62, 73
-er, -est **L5** 83
-s, -es, -ed **L4** 17

Long Vowels
/ā/*a-e* **L4** 18, 22, 28
/ā/*a-e (CVCe)* **L4** 51
/ā/*ai, ay* **L5** 13, 17, 20, 61
/ā/*ai, ay (CVVC)* **L5** 20
/ē/*e, ee, ea* **L4** 8, 12, 25, 75 **L5** 59
/e/*ea* **L5** 64, 68
/ē/*y, ie* **L4** 31, 35
/ī/*i* **L5** 23, 27

/ī/*i-e* **L4** 44, 48, 74, 82
/ī/*igh* **L5** 2, 6, 51, 58, 79
/ī/*y, ie* **L4** 78, 83
/ō/*o* **L5** 33, 37, 40, 76
/ō/*o-e* **L4** 89, 93
/ō/*o-e (CVCe)* **L4** 96
/ū/*u-e* **L5** 44, 48, 82

Phonograms
-ace, -ice **L4** 77
-ail, -ain **L5** 22
-ake, -ate **L4** 30
-ake, -ike **L4** 54
-ast, -est, -ust **L4** 66
-eat **L5** 84
-eed, -eet **L4** 43
-ose, -oke **L4** 100

R-Controlled Vowels
/är/*ar* **L4** 38, **L5** 71
/ôr/*or* **L5** 11

Vowel Variants
/ou/*ow* **L4** 67, 71

Skills and Strategies Index